#TOOSTRONG

*How to Win Fast and Win Often
in a World Full of Obstacles*

MIKE CLAUDIO

DEDICATION

To Corrado "Papa" Claudio, the man who
showed me with a dream, anything is possible.

TABLE OF CONTENTS

FOREWORD

I know a lot of really strong people. Seriously, two of my close friends have held world records for being the Strongest Man Alive, not to mention all my professional athlete friends and clients…

So, when I tell you Mike Claudio is one of the strongest people I know, that's saying a lot. Trust me.

Most of the super-strong people I know are only strong physically. For all the vigor in their body, they lack strength in their mind and relationships.

Mike is strong across the board. He's not just physically strong, but he's strong-minded, strong-willed, and a strong business builder.

As of the time of this writing, I've had the pleasure of being Mike's friend for about three years. We've done events together, planned business together, lifted weights together, and we talk about our families often.

I've observed Mike over these last three years and have watched how he moves and grows. First off, you will never see panic on Mike's face, no matter the situation. Outside of his strength, one of the things that I admire is his ability to always remain seemingly calm.

Another thing I love about Mike is his ability to take action. I can tell a lot about another man by how he performs in the gym. Mike is one of those guys who doesn't talk in the gym. He spends his time with his head down doing the work.

Mike is the same way in business. He's not all over social media bragging about how much money he's making (even though I know he makes a lot). He's busy doing what he has to do to make it work. He's tapped into his superpower focus and gets shit done!

Have you ever seen Mike's shoulders? They are huge! But not nearly as big as his heart. He set up his charity, A Champion's Shoes, and dedicates his time and talent to helping the kids who need it the most.

You're about to read a book that's as real as it gets.

No sugar coating.

No magic genie.

No handouts.

No lucky breaks.

Just a book filled with information on how to be strong in every area of your life. When you have strong relationships, a strong business, a strong mind, and a strong body, you can't be stopped. Force of Average be damned!

Mike's story is real, raw, and relevant to your life. You made a good decision in grabbing this book. Now keep up the good work and read the rest.

Ryan Stewman
Founder of Apex

P.S. Congrats on an amazing book, Mike. This is going to change a lot of lives. #WeAreApex

INTRODUCTION

*This book contains references to suicide and suicidal ideation. Please do not read it if you are feeling suicidal or are thinking of hurting yourself. Reach out to the National Suicide Prevention Lifeline: 800-273-8255

WHO IS THIS BOOK FOR?

This book is for the person who is struggling to get ahead. It is for the person who feels like they are missing that special recipe everyone else seems to have. The person who feels as though they are floating through life like a passenger. It is for the person who has yet to take control of their environment and their mindset to put them on the path of success.

I wrote this book for you because I want you to know the power of feeling like a winner is IN YOUR HANDS. I hope to give you the tools so you can build the life you want for yourself!

So, keep reading because I believe you can do it.

WHY I WROTE THIS BOOK

It was 11 p.m., December 28, 2019. I was sitting on the couch staring at a bottle of OxyContin pain pills, wishing it contained enough to end it all.

I had spent over a month in extreme physical pain and probably decades in mental and emotional pain.

I can't tell you exactly when the emotional demons started to grow, but the physical pain started right around Thanksgiving when I got an inguinal hernia. I won't go into the details, but it's NOT the belly button kind. On December 20, I had surgery to repair it.

I have had plenty of surgeries in my life from sports injuries, but this one took the cake!

And the worst part is it wasn't even caused by me heroically lifting a burning vehicle off a family or anything. I was literally just repositioning myself in a chair!

I have squatted over 500 pounds, deadlifted over 500 pounds clean, and jerked 375 pounds, but the final straw was shifting my body weight in a chair. I simply put my hands on the armrests of the chair in my office at the time to shift in the seat and pop. Double hernia.

I had squatted 315 for five sets of five that morning with no issues but moving my own ass was what did me in.

The worst part was I was sitting in front of a client. When I did it, I thought I had just shifted weird in my jeans since the area felt tight. And it had happened before, but this time was different. The pain was getting worse. Little did I know the true pain was just beginning.

The years and years of trying to be what others wanted me to be, of the dissatisfaction with who I was, what I represented, how I was approaching life, and what I had accomplished were all catching up to me, too.

Over the next 30-plus days, I spent every moment in pain. I was stuck with the hernia until I could have surgery, which I thought would bring relief. Well, I was wrong. That post-surgery pain was the worst of my life!

As usual, the doctor prescribed OxyContin for the pain. I believe that was the final ripcord that dropped the bottom out of the safe little box I had built for myself in my head.

For three and a half hours that night, I sat on that couch, looking at that bottle in the biggest coaching moment of my life.

Picture a table. On one side is a winey, sniveling, crying, beat up, broke down, drug addict, and on the other side is a confident, strong, military, head football coach figure.

In some messed-up way, I was playing both roles. I was emotionally empty, done, and ready to throw in the towel.

I was tired.

Tired of being in pain.

Tired of feeling lost.

Tired of feeling like I was letting everyone down.

Tired of feeling like I couldn't make anyone, especially myself, happy.

Tired of not being true to myself.

Tired of not being satisfied with the way I looked.

So, I sat there and bitched in my head.

"I can't go on like this," said the broken-down man.

"You are too strong to give in," said the coach.

"They would be better off without someone this weak," the broken man screamed.

"You are too strong to give up," said the coach.

"I would do it right now, but I am not sure there are enough pills to actually do the job, and I don't want to leave my family embarrassed," said the crying man.

"You are too strong to even try," said the coach.

"If it doesn't work, these pills will just put me in the hospital, and I will just end up with more medical bills."

"You are too strong to give in."

"I wish I could get to my gun."

"You are too strong to take the selfish way out."

"Who even cares if I'm gone?"

"You are too strong and have too much to accomplish to end it here."

For three and a half hours, this broken version of me battled with the coach in me. Over and over and over again, I told myself I was #TooStrong to give in and give up.

I was too good at what I do to not be here to create the impact I was meant to leave.

I was too strong to do this.
I was too strong to do this.
I was too strong to do this.

It felt like I was a spectator in this conversation, watching this calm, cool, collected, and confident version of me save the life of the weak and defeated me.

Eventually, the coach inside me talked me into waking up my wife Tiffany and bringing her into the conversation.

I could see the fear and confusion in her face, searching for the words to say, the questions to ask.

I knew she would be overwhelmed by it all and unsure where it all came from, but I didn't have a choice if I wanted to survive the night.

I watched her search her memory bank to find some experience she could pull from to settle into the role I just dragged her into unexpectedly.

Lucky for me, a year earlier, we had both listened to one of Ed Mylett's podcast interviews with a woman whose husband had died from suicide. Tiffany asked the questions we learned about from that interview.

She dug into what I was planning to do. How was I going to do it? Where was I going to do it?

Uncovering more of where my head was about the suicide than about what caused it was the quickest way to start to move through it.

It was a long few days and weeks after that.

Even days later, I was still on the edge. I was walking down the road, literally talking myself out of jumping in front of a moving car. I do not wish this scary shit on anyone.

But all I knew and all I kept coming back to was *I am #TooStrong to give up or give in.*

That's where the title of this book came from.

I believe I am #TooStrong to not reach my fullest potential and make the biggest impact possible.

I ended up getting professional help and taking the right medications to help regulate the lows, which helped a lot. I had a mental sickness, and with a lot of sicknesses, medication can be very helpful.

Every day got a little better, and I eventually got clear from it. But the biggest lesson I learned from it was to be okay with who I am and what I believe to be true.

This book is full of lessons that keep me in the driver's seat and help me stay healthy mentally, physically, and emotionally.

I will not be digging any deeper into the mental health struggles of this event. I truly believe it was a one-off issue that stemmed from a lot of pain and the added narcotics that pushed me over the edge. But it was a true rock bottom scenario: I really had to reevaluate what was important and start to make changes.

Without breaking and being able to refocus and relearn what is important to me, I would not have been able to win as fast or as often as I am today. I hope you will use this book to help you course correct your life and maybe even save it.

My experience proved that I had learned a ton of lessons over the years. I was able to use them to coach myself through that scenario. That pushed me into wanting to put those lessons into a book to hopefully help someone else along the way. Hearing and learning from other people's stories has had a major impact on my life, and I put this book together to share some of mine in hopes that you will learn YOU ARE TOO STRONG TO GIVE UP AND TOO STRONG TO NOT CHASE YOUR FULLEST POTENTIAL.

We are all #TooStrong to be held down by a single moment, distinct feeling, temporary emotion, or a person—if we declare we are. If we remind ourselves of our true power.

YOU are #TooStrong to lose!

There is hope that you can overcome whatever is facing you, and this book holds the proof.

I want you to know that you are not alone in your struggles. Plenty of people have conquered or even thrived through what you are in the middle of. That's because they had a way to combat their struggles and a powerful mindset to get them through it. You simply can't overcome anything you're facing without mental fortitude.

The mental strength to coach yourself through hurdles is another reason I wrote this book. I want you to have the mindset to give you an advantage in life no matter where you are or where you want to go.

A few of the primary lessons you will have in your tool belt once you finish this book:

- You will know how to plan, prepare, and execute your goals.
- You will know why it is so important to play to win instead of just playing to play.
- You will know how to fuel your mind and body to overcome life's obstacles.
- You will know how to build strong relationships and deliver on what you say you will.

Throughout this book, you are going to learn what I have done to help me think like a winner, dress like a winner, speak like a winner, and even build winning relationships. I want to help you develop systems and habits on your terms so you can change your mindset around what winning and losing look like and how to control both aspects.

Everything I share with you is what I learned the hard way. But you don't have to go down that path. I will get into a lot more of my story later in the book, all to benefit you. You can read through my real-life experiences, take the lessons from them, and implement them in your life. I use my stories to help paint the picture of what I experienced and how I took that lesson and turned it into a win later.

But more importantly, I want to share the lessons that were drilled into my head to save you the pain of learning the hard way on your own. As a business coach, it's important that I share every tool possible with you to give you an edge. My experiences will give you the lesson without the misery. If you pay attention and implement what I am about to teach you, you will see success in all aspects of your life!

You will also learn about how my experiences led to the perspectives I use to form my opinions on winning and the ways you can relate my lessons learned to your life so you can win, too.

I will share some of my family background that I think you will be able to relate to and how what I learned in my childhood contributes to my success today.

And since I am a business coach, naturally, we will cover communication, sales, business development, and leadership tactics. But I also believe that the reason we succeed in business has everything to do with how we live the rest of our everyday lives, how we structure our time in all aspects of life, how resilient our mindsets are, and what we define as a win or loss.

The book kicks off with a chapter on making a choice to win. I am sure you have heard the saying that we cannot control what happens to us, but we can control how we react to it. I think too many people hold on to past experiences that they think define their future outcomes. If you choose to see the events for what they are and not who you are, things become a lot easier.

Once you learn how to choose for yourself, Chapter 2 reviews what drives your will to win. Where does your motivation and discipline or lack thereof come from? You have to understand and firmly define your mission, your vision, and your "why" to weather the storms that will hit us on the journeys to come.

Then I am going to show you how to set yourself up for a winning streak!

You'll want to keep reading because Chapter 3 is the magic chapter. You'll learn how to prepare to win, how to turn a losing streak into a winning streak, and how to hold yourself accountable to keep it going. That's the basis of my Win Fast and Win Often mentality!

And before you get too deep into these pages, I want to stress that if all you take away from this book are the lessons in Chapter 3 about setting powerful goals to create winning streaks, you will have invested your time wisely!

But each chapter is chock full of good information to help you win in every area of your life. I wrote this book so that every topic ties into the next as you continue through the pages.

Chapter 4 will greatly help you understand the importance of creating that winning streak, not just for you but the people around you. Whether you like it or not, you are an influencer. You don't even realize that most of the people you influence are watching you and how you impact their lives.

Once you know what you are doing and why you are doing it, Chapter 5 will cover how to fuel yourself to win. It's not about just food and water but what information and influences you receive on a regular basis. Your mind craves more than your stomach does, and it's important to understand what you are feeding it to keep you on track.

It is also important to look the part. Leadership, success, and generally loving yourself all have a lot to do with how you look externally to others as well as internally to yourself. Chapter 6 lays out how to look good, feel good, and perform at the top of your game!

Once you are at the top of your game, it's important to use that power properly. Chapters 7, 8, and 9 covers the power of intentional and impactful relationship-building, how to become known, liked, and trusted, living a life of integrity by staying true to your word, and building strong relationships for the right reasons.

Chapter 10 takes a deep dive into the Rule of Reciprocity. On that note, let me just say that there are not enough people who give without expecting something in return. When you do this, it allows you to stand out easily. This is probably one of the biggest things I have focused on that has led to a lot of the success I have had. People do not expect you to come through for them without expecting something in return, so please implement what you read here, and you will immediately stand out from those around you.

If you have followed me on social media for any period of time, you know that follow-through and follow-up are at the core of what I talk about. Chapters 11 and 12 dive into how to set yourself up properly so you can follow through on what you say you will do, then follow up with others to guide them to do the same. Lack of follow through is one of the biggest frustrations in today's world. It doesn't matter where you are or who you are dealing with. When things don't meet your expectations or when improper expectations are set, your experience with that person or event becomes significantly worse. So, pay attention and implement, and people will not just like working with you; they will look forward to it because they can trust you will follow through.

In the final chapter, I will dig into how having a mentor or coach can change the trajectory of your entire life. I have spent tens of thousands of dollars on mentors and coaches, and each time, it has paid off for me. There are a lot of variables in finding and hiring a great coach that is right for you. I'll give you some of the insight I have learned going through the process from the client and the coaching perspective so you can pick the right one for you. If you want to learn more about me, check out www.winrateconsulting.com and my *Big Stud Podcast* on all major podcasting platforms, or connect with me on Instagram: @winrateconsulting.

THANK YOU!

I want to take a moment to thank you for making the time and financial investment into yourself to pick up this book and get started. I have heard it said before, and I genuinely believe this statement to be true: investing in yourself pays the most substantial return over time! You are here to take your first step toward getting ahead in life, or maybe you are already down the road of success and hoping to find an edge to win more consistently. No matter your situation, investing in yourself always makes sense. Whether you are experienced or are a beginner, the edge that you want can be yours. You just need to believe you can have it.

We all have our stories, and I want you to better understand some of the biggest things that have impacted who I am and how I operate so you can achieve everything you are capable of!

CHAPTER 1

MAKING THE CHOICE TO WIN!

It's not how hard you can hit;
it's how hard you can get hit and keep moving forward.
-Rocky Balboa

Feeling like a loser sucks.

But then the pain passes, and you learn from it. It's no different than how you feel when you get kicked in the gut—the pain always goes away. And the pain of thinking you aren't worth much because you messed up goes away, too.

After getting knocked down many times in my life, I have learned that losing is no more than an action, lesson learned, or mistake that requires you to analyze and adjust and sometimes apologize. You can encounter a lot of scenarios in life that do not show the best version of you. You can do something at work that gets you fired, try to play a new sport for the first time and feel out of place or like you are just bad at it because you've never done it before, or have a weak moment and yell at someone you care about because you are overwhelmed. While these moments of failure happen, they do not define who you are.

The real struggle comes when feeling like a loser becomes your identity.

This leads to a fear of rejection, fear of failure, and the internal false self-talk about what you think you are or are not capable of.

I've found an internal "coach" that gives you all the reasons you will fail is the biggest issue many people identify with. If you don't control that voice, it will begin to play a highlight reel of everything you have ever failed at to convince you that you cannot or will not be successful in whatever you are pursuing now.

For instance, maybe you tried to talk to that girl, or you applied for a job, and it didn't go your way. Now you think you can never try again. We have all either said it to ourselves or heard someone else say, "I could never do that." Or "I tried that once, and it did not work out." Then we got cold feet and pulled back to stay safe.

Imagine that you tried out for basketball in middle school but didn't make the team, so you gave up and moved on to something else. You likely missed a lot of what you could have learned and done successfully because the result didn't turn out the way you wanted right away, so you started to believe you were not capable. The truth is you were probably just ill-prepared. With some proper training and guidance, you could have made the team and played. In case you didn't know, Michael Jordan got cut from his high school basketball team. What if he had given up and said, "Basketball must not be for me."

We've all heard the internal voice that talks you out of something because the last time you tried that activity or aimed for that target, it didn't go your way. The most obvious case is how everyone at some point in their lives has been shot down by that girl or boy they asked out. Then you are hesitant to ever ask anyone out again. You don't believe that you can succeed, so you tell yourself a lie. If you have gone through this, maybe you've identified as someone who does not possess the qualities anyone would want. Maybe you still feel that way, and you have settled for someone who doesn't treat you the way you want, or worse, you are alone because you don't believe anyone would want to be with you. The issue is not with them. It's with you and your belief in the value you have and what you are capable of being.

Just because you have lost or are losing does not mean you ARE a loser. In its purest form, a loss is nothing more than a noun. It is a thing that affects you; it is not a thing that defines who you are! After years and years of anxiety and depression, of feeling lost about why I felt like a loser, I have learned that lesson, and I want you to know it too, so you will never get stuck in that mental trap again.

I will also share many other lessons that I have learned with you. I'll highlight the broader aspects of them in this chapter, and we will dive in more deeply as you progress through the book.

WE ARE ALL #TOOSTRONG TO LOSE

I now know I am not a loser, just as I was not a baseball player, student, or parent. I *played* baseball for a long period of my life, and I let it define who I told myself I was, but simply being on the field was an action I took. It was not my identity. If I was not winning on the field, I didn't feel like I was worth anything. The thrill of having a great game and getting all the glory that came with being a great player fueled me, but I let it become the only way I felt like I was worth anything regardless of other parts of my life I was doing well in.

I went to school and failed, but being a student was a season of my life. Failing did not define me. Actually, failing out of college was one of the best things that happened to me. A lot of the time, failure is pushed on us to allow us to move on from something we were not meant to do. I was not meant to be a classroom student. And to some people, that was a failure. But for me, it was an awakening. A lot of people I know let failing in school define what they were capable of in their future and how much money they could earn.

Parenting is another thing that can make you feel like you are failing all the time regardless of how hard you are trying.

Raising my five and three-year-olds is something I am doing, but it is not something that defines me. I love my boys, but anyone with children knows you lose more often than you win. You can't let feeling like you are losing with your kids stop you from doing what you are supposed to do. Just like one day your kids love hot dogs and the next day they are disgusted by them, they will change how they react to you on a daily basis. If you base your self-worth on the opinion of your kids, you will be set up for a roller-coaster of an existence in all aspects of your life.

You will always be a parent, but the level of success you feel in that duty changes wildly over time. Some days you have it 100% under control, and other days you feel like the worst parent in the world. The ups and downs of being a parent do not define you as a person, nor should you base how you feel about yourself on how a child is feeling about it.

What I have described to you are all activities that I participate in and want to be successful in, but they are not who I am because I will not be in one stage of my life forever. And what looks like a failure in one season will help you become a champion in another.

Being in a season of your life where it feels like you are losing all the time doesn't define you, and feeling like a loser does not make you one! You may be in a dead-end job where your boss does not appreciate you, but that does not define you. You may be in a relationship where you are feeling attacked all the time, but that does not define you. You may be following what you believe is right as the people around you make fun of you and treat you like you are stupid, but again, that does not define you.

I once heard a phrase containing a lesson that I wish I had learned earlier in my life. "What makes you an outcast in one season of your life will make you rise to greatness in another."

So don't let the people around you or the environment you are in at this moment define the type of person you want to be. OWN THAT SHIT AND KEEP PUSHING! There is not a single great real-life story of a hero who did not struggle at some point in their lives. Don't let your story end due to others' perceptions of you.

No one is a loser. No one!

This is a fact I have learned over time. Most, if not all, of my greatest attributes, skillsets, and mindsets came from overcoming losses. Some of those losses were much more significant than others. Regardless of how deeply they affected me, I am still here. Because I am still here kicking and screaming, I am going to tell you the stories of losing in the moment, so hopefully, you can avoid or overcome similar situations in your life!

I want to give you hope that losing is a single action that can roll right off your shoulders without turning it into a toxic downward spiral. What you do with losing is based on how you perceive it and the mindset you have about it.

If you view it as a lesson learned, you'll move on a lot more quickly than if you whined, complained, and beat yourself up about it.

Trust me! I know what I am talking about. I spent many years being unhappy because I had the wrong mindset around what losing meant! My incorrect perspective was why I was viewing many things as losses when, in reality, they were not.

I don't have a loss-focused perspective anymore, and because I refused it for myself, I know you can, too.

Maybe you were just never taught how to bounce back and use the lessons you learned to propel yourself further in life.

That's why I am starting my oldest son on this lesson early.

THE #TOOSTRONG MOVEMENT

When my son was four years old, we started the #TooStrong movement at our house.

After the incident where I wanted to take my life but was saved by my internal coach reminding me that I am #TooStrong to give in, I wanted my son to know that just because he feels down, hurt, or as if he failed, it doesn't mean he is a failure. It doesn't mean he has to stay in that place of frustration and hurt. He does not need to hold onto it and beat himself up or get discouraged by whatever happened. To give him a trigger of positivity when he gets whiny, frustrated, or upset, I yell, "HOW strong?" And he will scream back, "TOO Strong!" Then he'll beat his chest twice with his fist!

I do this with him because I want him to *coach himself up.*

I want him to be stronger than I was.

I want him to have the ability to coach himself through the tough times by reminding himself that he is #TooStrong to be held down.

I can't think of a better way to overcome what you are dealing with than YELLING, "TOO STRONG," AND BEATING your chest to remind yourself to stand up and overcome. Sometimes, you need that little jab to your brain to reassure yourself that you are more durable than the situation, and sometimes that reminder needs to come from yourself. Knowing that when my son feels down, he will hear my voice asking him, "How strong?" and that he will know he has the strength to overcome whatever his situation is—that's incredible!

The skillset of coaching himself through the lows will make him a person who can stand on his own two feet when I am not around—the goal of every parent. I am raising powerful and independent sons and giving them strong mindsets, so they can take losses as learning experiences and know they are #TooStrong to let anything hold them down. The ability to know they are #TooStrong to be controlled by their emotions or by other's opinions will allow me to send them off into the world with the tools to conquer any obstacle thrown their way. This is the greatest gift I can give my boys.

My kids are getting a head start. But if you didn't get one, it's not too late. Just keep flipping these pages.

THE CONNECTION BETWEEN YOUR WINNING MINDSET AND WINNING IN REAL LIFE AND BUSINESS

Now, let's talk sales. Or, more specifically, let's talk about winning in business. Learning to control your emotions and harness a strong mindset is what sets average and great people apart. If you have ever worked in sales, you know how challenging quotas, customers, and managers can be. It takes a special person to have a successful long-term career in sales because so much is working against you. I will touch on that concept in this chapter, but we are also going to discuss it to a much greater degree later in the book.

Every salesperson must do two things to be successful in their career. First, they must have worked in retail at some point, and second, they must have played organized sports. Now, don't go blowing me up if you know of examples where this is not the case. This is my opinion, and I believe these two factors are critical in helping you gain many skillsets. These two experiences had a massive positive impact on me. They taught me about handling the mindset that comes with that world. Even though those scenarios created depression and anxiety, they also brought me out of my struggles with them. You can't hide from your feelings in sports or sales, especially team sports and retail sales. If you cannot learn to be self-aware and control your mind, you will get chewed up, spit out, and not make it in those worlds.

You also have probably heard the phrase, "People buy from who they know, like, and trust." But what does that mean, and how do you make that happen?

Keep reading because I get granular on how to get known, liked, and trusted both in-person and online. To begin with, there is extreme power in doing what you say you will, in building strong relationships, and in following through. We've all been in those situations where we drop a ball that seems insignificant, but it might not be. As my dad always said, "It only takes one 'Ah shit' to kill ten 'Atta-boys!'" Man, if that isn't the truth. You can build significant trust with someone or even an entire market, but once you lose it, it is a challenge to gain it back.

Think about how much a bad review affects your business or how much your ex talking shit about you hurts your chances with your next relationship. Reputation is essential today because of how quickly people jump to judgment. Fair or unfair, you need to prepare for that, and I will help you get there! Having a bad reputation, being a person who can't be depended on, and being a person who is hard to like negatively affects your success and takes away your power to win.

WINNING IN RELATIONSHIPS, INCOME, AND HAPPINESS

How, when, and what to say to move the process along toward wins doesn't just hinge on sales. You need to focus on relationships, income, and happiness!

People will regularly forget about what they need to do as each task gets pushed down their priority list. It happens to all of us. We have the best of intentions to call that vendor or salesperson back, and then it doesn't happen. It's not because we don't want to; we just forget. You have to realize that your priorities are not always another person's priorities. When you are trying to close a deal with some-one, it helps to remind the other party involved that it's time to make a decision. Or you may need to tell them what must happen so they can accomplish their goals. Yes, sometimes it's best to walk away, but most deals can be salvaged when both parties are working together to find a solution.

Sometimes it just takes one more call, text, email, or even a meme. Believe me when I tell you there is a fortune in the follow-up if you are doing it correctly! I literally can account for over $4 million in sales directly related to following up. I'm telling you it's worth the effort!

It is not knowing this part of the process and the mandatory mindset needed to win that keeps most people down. But you will be lucky enough to have the tools necessary to control your routines and mindset because I'll give you the mental strength and self-belief to refuse to stay down and allow you to push through your struggles to reach a new winning streak. (Here's a hint: your winning streak starts with your next decision.)

YOUR GUIDING FORCE HELPS YOU DOMINATE

Knowing what decisions to make is one of the harder parts of success in life and business. Many times, you have to make decisions with minimal to no information, and what information you do have may not be accurate. But creating the vision and core values to guide you is vital and will help you to conquer this challenge.

Imagine being in a rowboat without a rudder. You can row your arms off, but you will never get to where you want to go because you do not have the rudder, aka the "guiding force," to keep you on track to reach a successful mission. You need to understand that your decisions impact more than just you or the immediate circumstances. They affect you, your employees, and your family in one way, shape, or form. You cannot captain your life's ship without the ability to guide it, or you will end up stuck and rowing your boat in a giant circle! Let me ask you: have you ever spent an entire year thinking you were working hard but, at the end, had nothing to show for it, so you started the new year off precisely in the same place?

Talk about feeling like shit!

WINNING LITTLE

Winning the little things is just as important as winning in the big picture! You can't go undefeated if you lose the first game. You can't accomplish a yearly goal in January. You have to be focused all year to make it happen. To feel accomplished, you need to know the difference between being busy and being productive in everything you do. You need to know how to reverse engineer your goals into manageable and trackable activities and how to reward yourself along the way to feel like you are winning. It's also important to know when you have finished a short-term goal and how to adjust a goal so you don't get burnt out! You will only accomplish what you plan to accomplish, and I want to help you learn how to figure out the planning aspect of reaching your goals!

HAVING A CHAMPIONSHIP MINDSET FOR LIFE

If you want to win all the way around, you have to do more than just create a plan. You have to know how to fuel your body, mind, and soul. This is crucial and probably the most undervalued part of our daily routines. The mindset of grinding your face off and working 25/8 without eating right, working out, and maintaining your mind won't work if you want to win consistently over time.

You may have noticed that a lot of "successful" people post about how they are out partying late and sleeping in. But between you and me, that just won't cut it either. Of course, it's fun to let loose occasionally, but it cannot be the norm!

When you want to reach goals, getting up early, eating right, working out, feeding your mind quality content, and preparing for the day so you can be ready for whatever life throws your way works.

You have to watch what you eat, too. Because you won't crush anything but the scale if you feed the machine garbage. Not to mention that if all you do is ingest crap, you will perform like crap. Conversely, feed yourself the best options, and you will operate to the best of your ability! It's not rocket science.

You get out of you what you put into you. Literally.

That's why I am dedicating some of this book to what works best when it comes to diet and nutrition. I will cover not only what and when you should eat but how—so you can maximize the fuel you put into your body. I am not a dietitian, and this is not meant to be an exact diet plan for you. It's a review of what I have learned works for me after trying every diet program in the book.

Once you have the game plan for what to feed your body, you'll also need to know how to look the part. If you don't look great, you won't feel great. If you don't feel great, you won't perform great! Period. There is no middle ground.

I will dive into exactly how to prepare yourself to look your best in every situation! Believe it or not, your body wants to perform better when you feel like you look good.

Think about what it felt like when you put on new shoes as a kid and how they made you run faster and jump higher just because they were fresh out of the box. There wasn't anything special about the shoes other than how they made you *feel* like you could do more kicks and leaps in them. And who didn't love walking into the first day of school with new clothes, shoes, and a backpack? (This is where the idea for my nonprofit, A Champion's Shoes, came from. Check out achampionsshoes.org to learn more.) *What makes you think you can walk into life in pajamas and Crocs!* If that's your uniform, you will approach the day feeling lackadaisical at best. And you won't take yourself seriously, which will make other people not take you seriously.

The bottom line is you are a creature of habit and environmental awareness. When you look in the mirror, your brain will operate with the tenacity or laziness it sees. Your brain interprets a game plan based on what you look like.

YOU ARE NOT TOO SMALL TO BE RELEVANT

The last few points of the book are quite possibly the most valuable part of your long-term strategy for success. Most of the people I lead and coach think too small and way too short-term. We all want to be remembered for a long time and to differentiate ourselves in a crowded environment. We want to stand out and for people to think of us as someone they can trust to help them. We want people to believe they can count on us when they need us, especially when providing that person value will also help you win. Your ability to decide when and how to implement your power affects people's opinions of you and is a central part of what makes people believe in you long-term. It plants the seed that will give you fruit in the months and years to come. You have to plant those seeds because it takes time for them to grow into something you can actually collect. The more seeds you plant, the more opportunities you have to be fruitful long-term.

THERE IS ONLY ONE THING IN COMMON BETWEEN EVERY SUCCESS STORY: YOU HAVE TO DO THE WORK IF YOU WANT TO GET AHEAD

Now that you are excited and prepared for what you are going to learn, I need to make an obvious point: everyone does not have the same needs. Everyone's story is different. Their timing is different. What may have worked before won't work now, and vice versa.

Everyone's landscape, market, family, or ecosystem is diverse, so it is valuable that you learn the strategies I am sharing. Don't be the person who calls out all the reasons why my situations and examples are different than yours. Instead, think of the reasons *why* I succeeded in certain areas where you haven't yet.

The first step to winning is to absorb information, pull a lesson out of it, and find a creative way to implement it into your situation.

If you are the type of person to point out regularly why something won't work before you think of a reason why it will, then it's no wonder you don't feel like you are winning. You're not permitting yourself to!

Here's a simple rule you can memorize right now: **you get what you focus on in life**. This means that if you focus on the reasons why your plan *won't* work, you'll get more circumstances where you don't win. But if you focus on why your plan *will* work, you will learn to be super creative in solving problems that lead to winning.

I am sure that you have goals, desires, and things you want in your life. And I am going to walk you through the steps I have taken to overcome some of my biggest challenges to find the wins in my life every day. When I put these strategies into play, it makes me feel less like I am losing and more like I am gaining ground on my goals!

JUST SHOWING UP TO COMPETE ISN'T WINNING EITHER

One of the practices that I want you to work on both in and out of this book is ignoring the people on social media that you compare yourself to.

Simply put, there is just no point, and you are never going to win because you are playing an imaginary game where people only show their highlights and hide from their darkness.

You already know that dealing with the pressures of today's environment is challenging enough when you are comparing yourself to everyone's highlight reel. I was that guy! (And I still kind of am sometimes.) That's how I also know engaging in the comparison game is a quick way to feel like a loser.

The age of social media has changed the game, not just in how we relate to and engage with others but also as it pertains to ourselves. How you view and judge what you have, how you look, where you live, and how you feel about the followers you have are all based on what someone else has that you feel you should have. And remember that people only tell you what they want you to know.

To view yourself as enough, you will need to break the habit of comparing yourself to others. You will need to define what success is to you and not allow anyone else to tell you your vision is wrong.

The first step in defining success your way requires you to ask yourself these questions:

- Who do you want in your life?
- What do you want in your life?
- Where do you want to live your life?
- What is the vision you want for your life?
- When do you want to reach the vision?
- How do you plan to get there?

> **These are all questions only you can answer.**
> **But what do they have to do with losing, you might wonder?**
> **The most severe form of losing is when you let *yourself* down.**

Ignoring the expectations you have set for yourself to please others is the quickest way to sink into an internal hole. I know the feeling of looking like you have it all together but hating life because you are not living true to yourself.

I am a guy who wears his emotions on his sleeve to an extent, but that is only part of what I deal with internally. I do my best to be prepared and look put together, but I have spent much of my life in a depressed or anxious state because I am worried about what others think.

I have been a great leader of others while being unable to lead myself correctly because I was so worried about letting people down.

I have been the top salesperson on a team but hated every minute of it at times because I never felt like I was doing enough in the eyes of the people who were important to me.

Almost all my mental struggles have happened because I put my happiness in the hands of others. The only times I have been okay or satisfied with a loss is when I know it happened because I did it my way. Any time I went about living my life based on what I thought others wanted from me was when the losses hurt the most and drove me deeper into whatever hole I was in at the time. I am far from perfect; I have just learned a lot about overcoming all this shit, and I truly want to help others do the same.

If you keep listening to others, the real unhappiness you will feel will be your conscience screaming that you are not delivering on what YOU want and need. If this is your case, start looking to yourself instead of social media influencers, motivational speakers, and maybe even your family for the validation that you are worthy of.

TRUST ME ON THIS ONE. Following your vision for what success looks like to you is the quickest way to happiness and to feeling like you are winning.

CHAPTER 2

WHAT DRIVES YOUR WILL TO WIN

Winning is not a sometime thing; it's an all-the-time thing. You don't win once in a while; you don't do things right once in a while; you do them right all the time. Winning is a habit.
— *Vince Lombardi*

Each of us is the sum of the decisions, experiences, and influences we encounter throughout our lives.

Our experiences allow us to look back and see how they have impacted who we are today. Good, bad, or indifferent, conscious, or subconscious, we are all unique. Some people use what has happened to them as an excuse for why they don't have more or why they can't accomplish what they truly want. Others use what makes them unique as their superpower to show the world they are capable of anything, which allows them to Win Fast and Win Often.

Which type of person are you?

OWNING YOUR SHIT

Kent Youngstrom is a well-known and skilled artist I met through CrossFit Weddington here in Charlotte. This dude is legit and paints for significant companies and celebrities. He also pushed me into starting WinRate Consulting. After talking to him for a little bit, he asked, "Why not start right now? What should the name be?"

And boom! Over one lunch, he helped me start my company—and even contributed to what the name should be. The rest, as they say, is history. What makes him so great at his craft is his ability to blend powerful, inspirational, and meaningful words into his art. (Check him out on Instagram to see what I mean: @kentyoungstrom.)

Kent has written one of the most powerful sayings that is found in a lot of his art. It reminds me that what we do, how we do it, and why we do it makes us all unique. As Kent says, "No one on Earth can do what you do precisely the way you do it." This means that we all have our unique fingerprint to leave on this world, and you are responsible for leaving that fingerprint where it matters most to you. Know that what you offer is valuable and own the shit out of who you are!

There are millions of reasons why we are the way we are, but I believe there are three very distinct things that have molded me into who I am today. In the previous chapter, I mentioned two things that have helped me the most in my life, but I didn't include my male role models. The back story about where I came from had a very powerful direct and indirect impact on my approach to life.

MY THREE SECRETS

#1: Stubborn Roots Run Deep

I am the grandson of an immigrant.

My grandfather on my dad's side, Papa, who this book is dedicated to, immigrated to the United States in the mid-1900s. Like most immigrants, he was wildly under-educated, having only completed the third grade. Papa didn't speak English or have any money, but he figured out a way to put four kids through college! He worked as a longshoreman in New York City for the majority of his working career, and he and my grandma, Nana, lived in an apartment in Hoboken, New Jersey, right across the water from New York—106 Willow Ave.

When I went back to New Jersey for Papa's funeral in 2021, I went by that apartment where it all started, and it really hit me how much strength and grit this man had to pull off building the family he had. One of the coolest things my dad told me about growing up was that from his kitchen window, he watched as the Twin Towers were built. When they went down in 2001, it was terrible, but I am thankful to have heard the flip side of the story from my dad—that he could see such fantastic engineering accomplished as it happened. That's a pretty cool story!

Papa was a no-nonsense kind of guy. He had every reason in the book not to be successful. With little to no money, zero understanding of the language, no friends or connections, Papa was dropped in the biggest city of a country he had never been to before. His is an incredible story of being #TooStrong to lose, especially considering all the other things going on in the mid-1900s, including the lack of technology and access to information.

As a result, my dad grew up in a pretty exciting environment driven by a no-bullshit, no-excuse mindset. For better or worse, I had a similar upbringing. My dad did a great job blending how his father raised him and how he raised us, but my childhood was still no-nonsense to a large degree.

If you wanted to be successful in New York City in that period when my Papa first came to America, you couldn't hang your hat on your excuses. You couldn't sit back and wait for something to happen. You couldn't whine or bitch about your circumstances. You simply woke up every day and did your job to support your family and protect yourself. He had a saying he used all the time: *Statevi d'accordo*. It means, "Stay the course and commit to the mission." I am sure many men and families feel and felt this way, but when a Claudio man gets an idea in his head, there is nothing and no one who will stop him. Anyone who knows a descendant of Corrado "Papa" Claudio knows we will outwork you, we will out-hustle you, we will out-plan you, and we will win. The funny thing is my dad has three sisters, and I wouldn't go up against them either!

The inside joke in the family is that when something isn't going how we think it should, you'll hear, "Okay, so here is what we are going to do!" That's when we know the person on the other side of that situation is in for some tough love. Typically, you know a power shift is happening when you hear one of my relatives say that. A few of my cousins and I laugh about it anytime we hear someone say it now.

Papa decided he wanted a better life, and when he immigrated to the United States, he didn't let anything or anyone stop him. He raised great and successful kids and made it his mission to give them a better life, which is why he did what he had to to pay for them to go to college. Everything he faced would have you shaking your head, saying, "No way he pulls this story off." But damn if he didn't make it happen. The best story to illustrate what happens when a man in my family makes a decision and how quickly he can execute it when he wants it badly enough revolves around how Papa and Nana met and got married.

When Papa decided it was time to get himself a beautiful Italian woman, he got a ninety-day visa to go back to Italy to fall in love, marry, and convince said beautiful Italian woman to leave everything she knew to come to America. Talk about implementing a self-defined deadline and making sure you didn't come back empty-handed! Within forty days, Papa met, married, and convinced my Nana to come back to the United States with him. I mean, *come on!* In today's world, if you are not swiping left or right (or whatever the correct direction is), you are not getting anyone's attention! Nana was 19, and Papa was about 25. That was in 1950. Sixty-six years later, they are still married. They raised four kids, have 13 grandchildren, and eight great-grandchildren with more on the way, all because of one stubborn Claudio man—all because two people fell in love and committed to making it work no matter what! Papa eventually passed on from old age and even in his final days and moments stuck to his age-old saying of *Statevi d'accordo,* making sure the family stayed together, focused on the mission of creating a better life at all costs. He is missed by many, but the impact everyone in his family tree is making will allow Corrado to live in action well past his death.

#2: Sports Are Priceless

The second thing that molded me into who I was as a kid and young adult was my involvement in organized team sports. Anyone involved in athletics, especially travel ball, will understand the value and lessons learned that stay with you for the rest of your life! Once you make the commitment to get involved in organized team sports, you have to come together as a group of strangers and work as one to accomplish a goal. You have to learn you can't win the season on day one and you must continually work on your skills to get in the game and stay in it.

I am sure that at some point in your adult life, you have been in a situation where you needed to work with a team to set a plan. You had to execute that plan while also continuing to work on your personal skillsets, so you would become more valuable over time.

As a kid, I didn't realize what I was learning, but as an adult, I know that was exactly what Little League taught me.

Team practice and games did not mean you didn't have to work on your own time to improve or find better coaches along the way for specific skillset improvements. Those who did the extra work got better and played at higher levels, while those who didn't never got better and eventually got cut or quit. So, why as adults do so many people think they can get a job and just pass the time without investing in themselves? If you think you can do your job the same way forever and eventually get a raise or promotion, you are sadly mistaken! It didn't work in Little League, and it won't work in your career where the stakes are higher!

The truth is, if you want to make the All-Star Team, you have to earn your place on the field when no one is watching. You have to put in the extra work, the extra swings, the extra running. Getting on the team doesn't happen without work. If you want to get promoted, you have to earn it in the same way. If you're going to grow or scale your business, you have to take the same actions that Michael Jordan, Tom Brady, and Tiger Woods do with their coaches to improve every day. *What will make you better than the competition?* It's the same thing that makes the superstars who they are. You have to hire a coach! It doesn't have to be me, but you will thank me later when you hire a coach who has been where you want to go because it will allow you to get there much faster without all the painful mistakes that come with the journey.

When you played travel ball or made an All-Star Team as a kid, you got to meet a bunch of kids and were told to play with them. You generally had never met these kids in your life, but in a short amount of time, you were all supposed to collaborate with the specific goal of winning whatever tournament you entered. This meant you needed to learn a whole new set of personalities, check your ego for the betterment of the team, and then you needed to be able to perform at your best outside your comfort zone! That was the only environment that a kid could play in when I was growing up.

When you joined a travel team or the All-Stars, more often than not, you went from being the best kid on your team to being just another great player on the field, which also takes getting used to. Then you needed to learn how to make friends faster and be comfortable with who you are! I did better sometimes than others but being in those circumstances forced me to learn how to be comfortable around people I didn't know, which, as you can imagine, has paid significant dividends in my career and businesses.

One of the biggest lessons I learned through years of playing sports is that you have to put in the work! You cannot win the championship on day one, and you are not guaranteed anything even *after* you sacrifice and put in the work.

Many people in today's environment are entitled, thinking: *If I do X, I deserve Y.* Anyone who has ever lost a championship game knows that is a bunch of bullshit!

You can do everything right all year—or for years—and one play, one lousy call, even coming up against a better team might cause you to lose. The sports gods don't care that you put in extra work. They don't care that you were the first one to show up and the last one to leave—which was my mantra. You only won when you were the best THAT DAY. Nothing leading up to that game mattered in the outcome if you didn't show up ready to perform and score more than your opponent.

This is an important lesson missing in today's environment where people believe "fair" plays a role in the outcome. Fair is not how life works. There is not a balance of how or why things happen to you or for you. If you are not the *best every single time* you compete, your chances of winning are not high. And in team sports, even when you are the best on the team, it's not all up to you. You can lose anyway. I had to learn to put in the work anyway, even if I didn't win. I had to learn to get up, dust myself off, and get back in the game!

I had to be strong enough to lose a game and return to do the work the next day, so I would be better prepared for the next opportunity. Ultimately, I found out that I am not entitled to anything. My chances of winning were and are determined based on my constant effort and how I continually focus on being 1% better every day. Giving up was never an option! It still isn't, and it never will be.

#3: Retail is a Teacher

The third and probably, the most powerful position I have had in my career that molded me and taught me some of my hardest lessons was retail sales.

When I landed my first retail gig, it wasn't a great time for me. As a young man, my life had been ruined.

Everything I had worked for was lost!

Or so I thought.

At the time, I was like any other high school athlete. I didn't simply have a dream of playing in college. It was the *only* option; there was no backup plan because it was all I had ever worked for. I didn't even have any other hobbies or activities I enjoyed other than sports. I had competition. That was it. On or off the field, I was always competing.

What I didn't have was a backup plan!

I will never forget sitting on the front steps of my house in Lynchburg, Virginia, after being injured and getting the call that my ACL was fully torn. I was going to need surgery plus a full six months of recovery. On the Sunday night before my senior year, I had been playing pick-up basketball with some friends when I jump-stopped awkwardly and completely tore my right ACL.

It was the fall of my senior year of high school. As a football and baseball player, baseball was my focus, and it was my best chance at playing at the next level. I'd decided to forgo my senior season of football to stay healthy and play in a competitive fall baseball league.

When I hurt myself, I knew I'd injured myself severely, but I'd hoped and prayed for the best! I mean, I go hard in the M-FN paint!

Then when I got the call from my doctor, I realized I had four months to do six months of recovery post-surgery. I was crushed. *Why me? Why now* was all I could think as I sat there on those steps.

In one night, I lost everything I was aiming to do with my life! I didn't have a plan without sports.

So, I fell back on what I always did and outworked the problem. I got my rehab done in three and a half months and was back to playing shape. I even went on to have a killer senior baseball season!

Then, in my last game of the season, I dove for a ball, my glove caught the ground wrong, and I tore the ligaments in my left thumb. As the pain ripped through my hand, I angrily thought, *give me a damn break!*

To make matters worse, I was known as a great hitter! Now, I couldn't even hold a bat!

I had to have another surgery and ended up going to Beach Week with all my friends in a cast and a metal rod sticking out of my thumb! Nothing screams, "HEY, LADIES!" like surgical equipment poking out of your hand.

But I solved that problem, too, and healed up. Then I played a year of college ball before failing out of school. Without realizing it, I had developed a drinking problem and got into a pretty deep depression.

At that point, I was out of sports, out of school, and out of options. I had to move back in with my parents.

I tell you all of this to drive home the point that I was #TooStrong to be defined by it.

I was #TooStrong to let anything stop me.

I was #TooStrong to let any challenge be the reason I failed in life.

I had a long way to go to get on my feet. I even doubted myself occasionally, wondering if I would ever amount to anything but a washed-up athlete who had potential but who had never achieved much. Still, giving up was never an option.

I know I am not unique or alone. Luckily, I realized that early enough to make a plan to come back.

You have also likely overcome some shitty situations and survived or even thrived through them. That's because you are #TooStrong to be stopped. You are #TooStrong to let whatever is happening right now be your defining moment.

Not graduating college was a big deal in my family. I knew deep down I was not meant to be a classroom student and college was not where I wanted to be. Nor did I want to go back into the environment where all I knew was failing classes, drinking heavily, and being depressed. So, I decided not to go back to school and turned that chip on my shoulder into a voice that said, "I will be successful without that piece of paper." But I was also living with my parents and didn't know what I was going to do. I did know I had to hang on and persevere in my belief in myself despite the fact I needed a job, I needed a direction, I needed a plan, and I needed to find a way to start winning again without sports.

Then one day, I got a call from a friend of mine asking if I was looking for a job.

Of course, I was!

The next day I interviewed with Alltel Wireless—now Verizon Wireless. That's where my sales career started. I don't know why I got the job because I flopped in the interview. Halfway through the interview, the district manager slid me a flip phone (this was pre-smartphones) and asked me to sell him a text messaging package. I had no idea what I was doing and had never formally sold anything in my life up to this point.

When I walked into the store manager's office, they had me sit at a conference table. I was seated across the table from the store manager with the district manager to his right. The district manager was a smaller guy with glasses who initially looked a little nerdy but ended up being one of the biggest hard-asses I ever met.

We did the typical interview small talk about my background and the role, then in mid-conversation, the district manager slid me his phone and said: "Sell me a text messaging package." (This was back before unlimited text messaging was a thing, and you had to purchase a text messaging plan based on how many messages you needed every month.)

Looking back, it was a genius interview tactic, but in my humble opinion, I failed miserably at accomplishing that request. As I sat there with the phone in my hand, I laughed and said, in an effort to demonstrate my selling technique, "Let me turn to my computer and see what packages we have available." Picture it: I literally turned around in my chair and pretended to click away at a keyboard. I am cringing while writing about this memory, thinking about what I would have done if I was on the other side of that table!

I left the interview having no idea what would happen next, but a day later, I got the job offer. They must have been desperate!

I will forever be grateful to E.W. Martin, the store manager, for giving me that opportunity. To give you an idea of how much he has cared for me since hiring me, he has not missed telling me happy birthday every year since I started working there! It's been over 15 years, and he has not forgotten one of my birthdays. And he is usually the first one to say it! He gave me the opportunity that would eventually shape the rest of my sales and leadership experience.

If you have ever been to a wireless retail store, you know it can be a war zone! Remember, I was selling before smartphones and before any online portal existed where customers could get information. I would sit or stand in that store for five to six days every week, dealing with anything and everything you can imagine.

People threw their phones at me and screamed and cussed at me. They even tried to fight me over their phone bill when they got charged for minute and text overages. Again, this was before unlimited everything was a thing. If I didn't credit text messaging overage charges to some customers, they would call me out to the parking lot to throw hands!

I was pretty much a child when I started working and selling wireless technology for a living and learned a lot over five years in the retail world before transitioning into the B2B (Business to Business) world for another four-plus years. Some of the most important lessons I learned involved dealing with an emotional client, overcoming objections, and planning for a quota that turned over every month. That meant I had to go from hero to zero every month! No matter how much I sold in one particular month, at the beginning of the next month, I started with zero sales and had to prove myself all over again. My bosses didn't care what I'd sold the last month; their only focus was, "How are you going to hit quota this month?"

I lived in that world for almost ten years. It was stressful, to say the least.

But the biggest lesson I learned in that environment was that if I wanted to win, I couldn't take things personally. That was also one of the hardest lessons I learned. Anyone who knows me knows I am an emotionally driven person, which made learning that lesson that much harder. I still take certain things a little more personally than I should sometimes, but back then, I took *everything* personally.

Over time, I realized that having empathy for the client and understanding where their frustration and anger came from allowed me to deescalate situations more effectively. It allowed me to prove that I was there to help them, *not battle them.* I also figured out that people were not mad at me specifically. I was the face of Verizon to them, and they needed to vent. Since I was the target, I had to take that role seriously.

Once I got a handle on that lesson and skillset, I realized how much easier it was to help clients buy. Turning the corner on my mindset and approaching each client's situation with empathy not only helped me overcome challenging clients, it also helped me become a much better salesperson.

I discovered why clients made decisions, what drove them to specific products over others, and what problems or needs made them decide to come into the store. I used a more consultative approach to truly understand what problem the client was trying to solve and what features they wanted. The moment I wrapped my mind around where they were coming from, it turned me into a selling machine.

The basis of almost all my sales success starts with my ability to better understand what problems my clients are trying to solve. This is more impactful than knowing what products or services they believe they need. I use what I learned from those early days of selling even today.

When I worked at Verizon, I built relationships with people and their families. I connected with them so I could understand the root cause of their problems and push them to overcome them. I didn't just ring them up for what they *thought* they needed.

I guided my clients to the right solution for their problem versus helping them find the cheapest option.

I learned how to present questions differently to get better answers.

I learned the power of image and how people treat you differently based on what you are wearing and how you carry yourself.

I learned that you have to show up every day and do the work. If I wanted to make money, I had to sell.

I learned not to judge a client before digging into their situation—because you never knew who would bring you your biggest deal of the month.

Anyone who has worked retail knows you judge a client from the time they pull into the parking lot. It's easy to develop an opinion based on how people look and carry themselves. I had to unlearn that habit. In doing so, I stopped shying away from clients because they didn't *look* like a buyer. In fact, I got that perception wrong enough times that I started treating every client the same. That's how I figured out that you never knew who your best client would be and who was going to waste your time.

This is a lesson that I preached to the employees I had and to the clients I coach now. To this day, I still surprise people with how powerful this change in mindset is!

Remember, you are always one call, one email, or one DM away from your next best client or referral partner. The only failure is quitting. So, if you are in a sales slump right now, remember you are #TooStrong to stop!

These lessons allowed me to differentiate myself for the rest of my career.

Approaching sales from the perspective of how people make decisions and for what reasons changed the game for me. Coming at it from a perspective of empathy allowed me to start building much stronger connections and relationships with people. When I began to learn more about my clients and got to know them on a personal level, it made me love what I was doing even more because I truly was helping people at a much deeper level!

SALES LESSONS BECOME LIFE LESSONS

Don't let your circumstances define you. Don't let anyone, including yourself, tell you what you want is not possible. If my grandfather can immigrate to the United States, work his ass off, and put four kids through college, you can do anything you put your mind to.

All you have to do is decide what you want and then don't let anything stand in your way.

If you are uncomfortable around new people, learn to be comfortable. Whether you are networking, at work, or in public, everyone feels a similar sense of discomfort when they are around people they don't know all that well. So, be yourself, and you'll be surprised to learn that you will Win Fast and Win Often!

Realize that you need to put the work in regardless of the outcome. Control your efforts and never stop striving for better ... both in business and in life. Understand that winning is not guaranteed, but the struggle is, so embrace the struggle and fixate on consistently working your plan.

Approach all the people in your life with more empathy. Seeing things from other's perspectives and circumstances will make you a better communicator, salesperson, leader, parent, and friend. The more you can understand where someone is coming from, the easier it will be to guide that person to where they really want to go calmly and with less reactive emotion!

Finally, don't just read this chapter and say, "Damn, those were a lot of great lessons!" and then move on.

Before progressing to the next chapter, I want you to write down two or three things that you are going to implement in your life and then create a plan to make it happen! Don't just list out what you are going to do. Get specific and note both *what* you are going to do and *when* you are going to do it. Make the plan specific and use deadlines and deliverables. Commit to making this a priority and hold yourself accountable or find an accountability partner. If you need one, shoot me a DM or tag me in a post on Instagram: @winrateconsulting.

As I have mentioned, letting yourself down is the biggest loss you can take, so don't let this be another notch on that belt. Make a change and take the steps to move forward—no excuses!

My life story cannot fit into one chapter or even one book—and it is not the content that I most want to focus on. But I wanted you to get an idea of where some of my best life lessons came from. I thought it was important to provide a little background and credibility as to how I became the man, coach, mentor, friend, and father I am today. I will pepper in additional lessons throughout the book, but I suggest digging into my *Big Stud Podcast* as well. Just search "Big Stud Podcast" on whatever player you use most. If you don't have one, the show can be found easily on Spotify, Apple, or in the link in my Instagram bio.

We all have things we want to accomplish or a vision for what we wish our life would be. We also know that wishing alone won't get us where we want to go, so in the next chapter, I am going to go over the steps of how to set goals and maintain accountability through completion.

There will be bumps in the road, of course—that's life! When you start to fall off the track or find yourself in a rut, get back on the right path by creating a winning streak. I am sharing more about how to do that in the coming pages, so make sure you keep reading!

CHAPTER 3

POWERFUL GOAL SETTING CREATES WINNING STREAKS

If you fail to plan, you are planning to fail!
—Benjamin Franklin

It has never been harder to feel like a winner than in today's world.

But it has also never been easier to win.

The entire image of what it means to win has been messed up by a market that is driven by what is the newest, flashiest, most exotic thing that you *don't* have. Each year, the world has to one-up itself to keep growing, making money, and expanding on technologies and advancement. But for this aim to work, the system has to be built to make last year's model appear obsolete.

That is why a new iPhone comes out every year and why people stand in line for days to get it even though not much has really changed since last year's version. We are taught that if we are not advancing with the times, we will be left behind and become obsolete. You see this in the technology and travel industries. You see this in the health and fitness industry as well.

Remember when we used to hear about 30-minute abs, then it became 15-minute abs? Now, you can wear specific equipment that will flex your abs "FOR ONLY 30 SECONDS A DAY!"

The way people and businesses portray the image of what people want their lives to be is so simplified. We have broken down the message to be one that tells us all we need to do to win is be better than last year's "BEST MODEL EVER." It's gotten to the point that we are now lost and confused about the work it actually takes to win.

- You see this happen on HGTV shows that inform you that 30 minutes and $15,000 is all it takes to get a kitchen remodel. You see it with on-line business coaches touting that you must follow their 30-day plan to make six figures a month as they did. You see it with every damn diet plan ever created! We are being fed the message of, "Do this simple task years to get fat, this 60-day strategy will get you ready for this incredibly short amount of time, and even though it took you five beach season."

The message sounds great, but it doesn't work!

It takes consistent work over a long period of time to truly be successful and reach your fullest potential. But when we believe the message we see, try it, and it doesn't work, we beat ourselves up and say stupid shit, like, "I guess I am just not meant to be fit." Or we say, "I am not meant to be wealthy." You are being lied to on a regular basis about what it takes to actually win in a sustainable way.

On the flip side, it has never been easier to have an idea, find information to implement it, launch that idea, get access to people who want to buy that idea, and scale your idea. Anyone can start a business at any time in this country. Anyone can get access to potential clients or information and opportunities to improve their idea. Starting a new business has never been easier, but easier does not mean easy.

That said, can you imagine taking an idea and creating something like Ford, Coke, or GE without the internet? It's far easier to get a business off the ground today when you look at what businesses in the past had to do to gain a foothold.

The truth is, the harder many of us try, the more we beat ourselves up because we've found out that winning is not as easy as we believed it was going to be.

News flash! Winning is nowhere near as simple as people show it to be! I am going to give you a brief lesson on why I believe this is the case—and I'll even throw in some sales advice.

IT'S ALL ABOUT HOW PEOPLE ARE DESIGNED

People make decisions based on emotion.

If we do not feel we will be happier by doing something, we just won't do it.

But the fact that action is driven by emotion is not a new human process. In fact, marketers understand this better than anyone. Companies and influencers alike excel at making their audience believe they are not performing at their optimal level because they don't have the product, service, or message that they are promoting. Products we never wanted or needed are thrown in front of us strategically with the message that you are not good enough without it! This is done because without making you feel like last year's version isn't good enough and you wouldn't be your best self without it, marketers would not be able to sell you this year's version. In a sense, marketers have to prey on you to stay in business.

Think about it.

If you are continually fed information through TV, radio, print media, and social media that you are not as good as you could be, you'll eventually tell yourself that you'll be better off with that thing you don't have yet. You will start to believe that you are unhappy with what you have, and it'll force you to buy something to fill a hole that was created by the advertising. Once that belief is stuck in your head, you'll believe it, even though it's a lie. When you recognize that you believe it, I challenge you to take time to show gratitude for what you do have in your life. It's likely that the thing you now are unhappy with was a dream you hoped to achieve one day. Whether it's the house, the car, the body, or the partner, at one point, something you have that isn't making you happy was something you dreamed would be possible one day.

Social media represents the worst of this messaging because, on social media, it's not just companies that want you to believe you are not as good as you can be. You'll find a bunch of people who want you to believe they have it better than you. Fake money, rented cars, high-end Airbnbs, beaches, and getting the perfect angle for the perfect picture that you see all over the place drives home the message that you are "less than." The highlight reel of people's lives showing the ideal family or the most magnificent vacation ever, is shoved down your throat on the daily.

But what these people don't show you is their miserable weather, how their kids never listen, or that their spouse is a workaholic who's never home.

> **This slide show of excellence is the lens
> we are watching the world through now.**

It's created to make people's stories seem better than they are, so you will wish you had whatever they are selling!

No wonder so many people struggle with the image of what it takes to win. No wonder they believe it is far harder than it really is. They are holding themselves up against competition that is likely not even real or, at a minimum, not the full story.

> **Too many people have put the measuring tool of
> what winning looks like in the hands of people whose
> job it is to make them feel like what we have isn't enough.**

What could go wrong there?

How about losing our grip on our self-validation?

This constant parade and roller coaster of what will supposedly make you happy compared to what made you happy in the past—but doesn't anymore—has created a mental health epidemic that no one talks about. The less happy we are, the more money we spend on stuff we don't need to impress people we don't care about, resulting in us never feeling satisfied or fulfilled. The fundamental equation that most of the market is basing their success on is this: reducing happiness promotes more spending, and more spending puts more money into the pockets of the marketer that can make you the happiest.

When you look through this lens that is different than what you normally perceive, do you see how people can get into the tailspin of never feeling like they can get ahead?

I hope to use this chapter to redefine what winning can be like for you and how to set up your life for real success.

HOW TO ACTUALLY WIN

The quickest way to start winning is to align with the right scoreboard. In other words, you need to know: what are you using to judge your success? If you are basing your success on the unrealistic expectations of getting what you want quickly, you will fail every day.

As mentioned above, the sales and marketing community have built a world around showing you what you *don't* have.

Now consider this: if you don't measure today's you against yesterday's you, even your wins won't feel like wins. Simply put, you won't see the progress because you won't be keeping track of it. If you want to know how far you've come, you need to assess it.

KEEPING TRACK OF THE LEAVES

When I was a kid growing up in Pittsburgh, Pennsylvania, my brothers and I were blessed to have a batting cage in our backyard courtesy of my dad and uncle. Every fall, when the leaves would hit the ground, and it got too cold to be outdoors hitting, we would take the net down and lay it out in the driveway to get it folded up and stored away for the winter. But before we could do that, we would have to make sure all the leaves were out of the net so they didn't deteriorate the fabric while it was stored.

We would start on one end of the net and pick out one leaf at a time and work down the entire length. Eighty-plus feet doesn't seem that long until you have to pull out what feels like millions of leaves. We always wanted to squeeze in as much practice time as we could, so we waited until the last minute before the season turned and all the leaves were down. Then when we would take the net off the frame, and it would land on the ground. The net was too heavy to carry and keep it off the ground, even though we did the best we could. Once it was on the ground, we would drag it from the backyard to the driveway—of course, picking up a lot more leaves. Imagine a Western Pennsylvania split-entry home surrounded by trees dropping an incredible amount of leaves every year! It made for great leaf piles for us kids to jump into, even though dealing with the net full of leaves was a pain.

My dad would always get my brothers and me to help with the net, and every time we would bitch about how many more leaves we had left to pick out, Dad would remind us to look back and see how far we had already come.

When we looked back, we would see we had done more than we realized. Seeing our progress would make us feel a little bit better about what we had done. I'm not saying it stopped the bitching because kids suck sometimes, but the lesson learned was that sometimes you need to look back at how far you have come to realize how much you have accomplished.

Looking back at the net of your life and seeing how many leaves you have pulled out is incredibly powerful when it comes to how a lot of us measure ourselves.

We spend so much time looking forward, chasing the "finish line," and killing ourselves to solve every problem or obstacle thrown at us that we never take the time to appreciate the progress.

I have been preaching for years about the benefit of falling in love with the process and that the results will follow. The process I am talking about is whatever is necessary to do each and every day to get the win. It could be a sales process, a health and fitness process, or even a study and learning process. It doesn't matter what the process is. My point is that you cannot win without doing the daily tasks necessary to keep momentum and create wins daily. I have measured myself and anyone who has worked for me based on how well they are following the process more than the direct results because results will come and go, but a reliable process will always win in the long run!

The problem with only measuring results is that people have terrible attention spans. Every time we see something a little better, nicer or shinier, our end goal changes, moves, or gets bigger!

I can say from experience that the pattern looks like this: you are down the path of winning, having made progress, but every time you hear or see something better than where you were before your vision changes. Then you give up on the game plan and pivot. The problem is if you are constantly changing your end goal, you will never feel like you are winning. That would be like changing your major every year and starting over on a different educational path. Not only does that take a lot more time, but it also costs a lot more money.

Yes, it is necessary to pivot sometimes, but only when you are basing that decision on what you genuinely want, not on what the world is telling you that you *should* be wanting.

After reading all that, you might be wondering, *but Mike, how do I fix my broken ways?*

Well, it starts with creating the goals or visions that are directly connected to what you want. Having that level of granular clarity is incredibly powerful. If you only set giant, lofty goals—which are essential, of course, but not the only goals you need to set—you'll never know if you are winning along the way. You need to set smaller goals that lead to larger ones.

When I have tried in the past to build out a larger goal, people would say things to me like, "Describe your perfect life," or "Describe your perfect day." But I have always struggled with doing that.

I don't jibe with this concept because one of my best strengths of setting super big goals is also a weakness.

Every day, my hours are incredibly structured. I create such a routine that I think in terms of one task to the next, one day to the next, and one week to the next. Then, because I have fallen so in love with the process and know if I follow it, I will win, it's hard to stop that grind. When it comes to what I am looking to accomplish ten, 15, and 20 years from now, it is hard to picture.

Another reason I struggle is that I battle internal demons and negative self-talk about the dreams I have. I will think, *I want a big awesome house on a lake with a killer infinity pool and a basketball court for the kids.* Then I will immediately think, *maybe it's not for me.* I know when I entertain thoughts like that, if I don't get my next task done, I'll never reach the finish line. Yes, I know I have to stay incredibly productive and ready for opportunities, but I still struggle with visualization and actually believing what I want to do to be possible.

But I think a lot of people struggle to identify what it is they truly want or what real success looks like. So, the good news is that you are not alone. The other good news is that there is a way to get to where you want to go.

In struggling with this challenge, I read *The Magic of Thinking Big* by Dr. David Schwartz. Since his process outlining the Ten Years' Planning Guide helped me a lot, I figured I would share it with you. And yes, it has everything to do with chopping up your larger goals into smaller bites to make them easier to attain.

Dr. Schwartz's process is pretty straightforward. If you implement it well, the rest of the chapter will have a lot more meaning for you Here's a breakdown of Dr. Schwartz's process.

TEN YEARS' PLANNING GUIDE

(Before you begin this exercise, I would start a note on your phone or computer so you can either copy and paste out what you wrote and then reference your answers if you need them. DO NOT SKIP THIS EXERCISE.)

A. Your Work Department - Ten years from now:

These are the crucial questions that you need to answer:

1. What income level do I want to attain?

2. What level of responsibility do I seek?

3. How much authority do I want to command?

4. What prestige do I expect to gain from my work?

B. Your Home Department - Ten years from now:

1. What standard of living do I want to provide for my family and myself?

2. What kind of house do I want to live in?

3. What kind of vacations do I want to take?

4. What financial support do I want to give my children in their early adult years?

C. Your Social Department - Ten years from now:

1. What kinds of friends do I want to have?

2. What social groups do I want to join?

3. What community leadership positions would I like to hold?

4. What worthwhile causes do I want to champion?

If you sincerely believe in this exercise and take it seriously, it allows you to stop comparing yourself to what you see and hear everywhere else. You will measure your success and wins against *your* vision—the vision you create by completing this questionnaire. These answers will be your guiding light to hold yourself accountable to the process necessary to get you where you want to go.

Make sure you answered the questions using your wants and desires and not what you think others will think of the way you explained yourself. If you need to, go back, reread your answers, and make sure that what you have recorded matches your vision. Remember, your friends and family and even your mentors are not in control of your happiness. Only you can decide what will make you happy!

Completing this exercise will also allow you to create better steppingstones both for the short term, mid-term, and long-term to ensure that you will stay on the right path!

My wife Tiff and I struggled with setting short-term goals for years before we found a solution we could stick to and use effectively. Before we switched gears to this process, we would say things like:

- "Let's save more money this year."

- "Let's lose some weight this year."

- "Let's go to church more this year."

These are all great ideas, but they are impossible to accomplish because they are not tangible, measurable, or trackable.

Well, all of that has changed for the better for us. Now, we set specific goals for specific parts of our lives.

After years of trial and error, we have hit upon a successful method that I want to share with you. Below is a breakdown of how we set goals for ourselves and our family. You can apply this to you and your family as well.

BREAKING DOWN YEARLY GOALS

On December 31 every year, my wife and I each choose a word for the upcoming year that we use as our guiding focus to help us accomplish specific goals.

In 2019, my word was "harmony" because I wanted to work on finding more work-life harmony. Understand that I don't believe there can be a work-life balance, but there can be harmony. Tiff's word for 2019 was "intentional" because she wanted to get a lot more intentional in her decision-making and actions.

Our words for 2020 were "rise" and "elevate." Tiff chose "rise" because she needed to rise to her expectations better this year. I chose "elevate" because I wanted to focus on elevating my entire client experience. Even as the pandemic threw us all for a loop and my business was affected, we stuck to these words as our focus which kept my head down on the mission instead of looking at what was going wrong around me. I was able to implement a lot of new strategies and services that created an elevated client experience throughout the year and into 2021.

Then we set goals for the following year based on our main categories of focus (that I will get into below):

- Love
- Home
- Family
- Spiritual
- Financial
- Physical
- Career

We tried to make these goals as measurable and trackable as possible.

Below is what our 2020 goals and accomplishments look like. You can use these to get an idea of how to build out your own plan:

MIKE'S AND TIFF'S 2020 GOALS

Words

- Mike: Elevate
- Tiff: Rise

Love

- Date night twice a month
- Dance lessons
- Using Love Dare, a book that guides you through a 40-day challenge with a new dare every day
- Sexy time weekly
- Weekly appreciation, like sharing cards, little notes, flowers, a homecooked meal, or just watching the kids so the other can have some quiet time

HOME

- Install storage shelves for Christmas decorations
- Family pics—get them hung around the house
- Minimalist mindset approach to spending money on things in our life. (I highly suggest doing research on the minimalist approach if you are trying to get more financially set in life)
- Festive wreath and decor for every season

FAMILY

- Yearly books—we create a book for every year of the kids' lives using pictures we took throughout the year so we can look back and see how they have grown over the years

- Sort pics

- Weekly family nights

- Monthly date nights with each boy

- One new experience per month—this could be anything we have never done before, such as taking a cooking class, going ax throwing, painting, or signing up for an art class

- Family pics—get new ones taken

SPIRITUAL

- Read through the Bible

- Make church a priority

- Pray with the boys weekly

FINANCIAL

- Tithe savings

- Move at the speed of cash—meaning if we don't have the cash to buy it, we won't buy it. We have struggled with credit card debt and are making a conscious effort not to get back into old habits this year. In 2019, we paid off over $120,000 in debt—mostly student loans—but a good chunk of credit cards as well. We don't want to go back down that rabbit hole.

- Weekly cash flows

- $0 credit card debt

- Stretch Goal—three months of expenses in savings

PHYSICAL

- Renew You Challenge—this was a challenge that Tiffany wanted to accomplish through one of her groups
- 20,000 mins of exercise
- Live Hard challenge–the four phases including 75 Hard that Andy Frisella created
- Half-marathon
- Ten-miler

CAREER

- 15,000 minutes of reading
- $500,000 in revenue—WinRate
- 30 1:1 coaching clients
- 100 online courses sold
- 12 speaking engagements
- Write a book—clearly, not all targets get hit. I started the book in 2020 but ended up finishing it in 2021
- Arete live event
- Rise business event
- Get published in one magazine every quarter
- Make Plexus fun—Plexus is a gut health supplement MLM my wife sells part-time
- One million downloads on Big Stud Sales podcast (It's cool to have some wild and outlandish goals, too!)

ENGINEERING DAILY TASKS

Once you have written down your goals for the year in each of the categories, you'll engineer the daily tasks you need to execute. Take the big goals and break them down into daily or weekly tasks you need to complete to hit your targets.

For example:

- 20,000 minutes of exercise for the year equates to 55 minutes a day.
- 15,000 minutes of reading for the year is 42 minutes a day.

Those are easy equations.

Now let's say you want to bring home $100,000 as a business owner. In this case, it's a little more complicated, but it's still easy to do if you know your numbers.

In the following equation, I am using the assumption that you have a 10% net profit margin and a 40% close rate with an average project size of $15,000.

That means …

- To attain $100,000 home-based income on a 10% net profit margin, you need to gross $1 million in revenue.

- To attain $1 million in revenue based on average client sales of $15,000, you need to close 67 clients.

- To sign 67 clients at a 40% close rate, you need to prospect 168 clients.

- If you are disqualifying 25% of the leads you are getting, you need to get 224 leads.

- Assuming it takes five prospecting calls or emails to acquire a lead, you will need to make 1,120 contacts for the year.

Then you can break the yearly target down into more manageable pieces.

For example, you can derive that you need to make 22 contacts a week or 4.5 connections Monday through Friday to bring home $100,000 per year.

Having a measurable daily target of what you need to do to accomplish the goal seems pretty attainable, doesn't it? I guarantee your wins will happen daily by focusing on and identifying and recording your four to five contacts instead of saying, "How on earth am I ever going to sell $1 million per year?"

That's no kind of plan, and so it will get you nowhere.

A QUICK SIDE NOTE ON HOW I DEFINE "BEING ON THE GRIND"

Many people define "being on the grind" as working your face off 25 hours a day, eight days a week. That equates to no fun, no family time, no travel, and no nothing other than the grind! Is there a time and place for that sacrifice? YES!

But I define grind as breaking a large item into smaller bite-sized or manageable pieces. Think about a pestle and mortar. When you use them, you're grinding a larger piece down into a more manageable and consumable size. Grinding out your goals allows you to manage them rather than biting off more than you can chew!

What I have learned through following this process is that anything I commit to doing and hold myself accountable to complete is a win.

Whether it is making my bed every day, the five daily contacts I secure, 55 minutes of exercise, 42 minutes of reading, eating better one meal at a time to lose weight, or making sure I kiss my wife goodbye every day when I leave the house, so she knows I love her, I can control every one of those things. You can plan and track everything in your life, too.

It's honestly that simple.

The bonus when you do this is that you will gain the confidence you need to keep winning. You will do this by committing to yourself that you will follow through on completing your daily tasks. When you learn you can hit your goals, it fills you with the confidence to do more … and so you do more. That enables you to build onto smaller accomplishments that lead to your biggest wins. If you focus on yesterday or tomorrow, you literally cannot achieve success because you have no control over the past or the future. So, you have to focus on today only. You do have control over that!

Most of us are good at committing to others and following through on what we tell them we will do. If your boss asked you to do something, you would take pride in completing that task. If a friend asked for a favor, you would follow through and show your friend that you appreciated them. If someone in your family needed something, you would take ownership to make sure they got whatever they needed.

Why don't you hold yourself to the same standard when you decide you are going to do something for yourself?

Why do you give up on the goal, the diet, the workout, the laundry, the yard work?

Wins are simple, but it's hard to hold yourself accountable consistently. Did you know an act as simple as making your bed every day can change the course of your entire day? And that changes the week, which changes the month, and so on and so forth.

Still, even if you decide right now that you are going to commit to yourself, does it mean that you will never encounter another moment where completing your tasks is difficult?

No.

Of course, not.

So, what do you do when you feel yourself slipping or getting away from the habits, routine or daily activities necessary to get to your big goals?

REMEMBER TOMORROW

One of the best lessons I learned to correct myself when I started to slip is Remember Tomorrow.

This lesson originated at a live Arete event in 2019 that I missed because I'd had surgery the day before and couldn't fly. I was bummed because I really wanted to meet all the great people who I have only met over the phone or through social media. Luckily for me, Arete offered a live stream of the event, and I could watch it from home.

If you don't know what Arete is, it's an entrepreneurship program run by Andy Frisella and Ed Mylett. Take my word for how effective this network is and look into it! At the event, Jesse Itzler gave a speech, and a good portion of it was on his concept of Remember Tomorrow. It was the first time I had heard Jesse speak live, but I felt that since he had started, grown, and sold businesses to

Warren Buffet and Coke, he seemed like a guy to listen to. I'm not saying Jesse knows everything, but he knows *a lot* about setting and achieving goals. So, I paid attention.

The premise of Remember Tomorrow is to think about how you will feel about the decision you are going to make tonight when you wake up tomorrow.

- Is that drink worth it?

- Is missing that workout worth it?

- Is taking that person home from the bar worth it?

- Is not getting your prospecting or social media content done worth it?

I am sure we have all woken up and said, "DAMN, I wish I would (or would not have) done that (insert decision you made the night before)."

I am sure I am also not the only one who has woken up after a night of partying and said, "I am never drinking again!"

When you are trying to talk yourself out of something you know you need to do or when you are telling yourself you deserve a night off or a few extra drinks, remind yourself about Remember Tomorrow. Assess if you still think the decision you are about to make is a good idea. In addition to remembering tomorrow, remember, you are #TooStrong to talk yourself out of what you know you need to do!

Still, you may encounter a day when you get off track or are just in a funk, a day when even Remember Tomorrow might not shake you out of your mood.

When that happens, you need to create a winning streak. It is amazing what a winning streak can do for you! It is amazing how one win can turn into a habit just as much as a loss does. This is the way that a streak happens, one win at a time. Or … one loss at a time … but we don't want to go there.

HOW TO CREATE A WINNING STREAK

There are two main parts that make up a winning streak that you need to remember and use. First, you need the right perspective. Second, you must focus on the actions you can control.

If you are feeling out of it and as if you can't win at anything, simplify your tasks and look at them from the perspective of what you have control over. Getting upset about the traffic making you late, or how the weather is stopping you from getting something done, or what your team or leadership has done to impede your success is not helpful because you can't control any of those things.

Remember that losers look at what others have done to slow them down, while winners look at how they can maneuver around obstacles and still win.

The only things you can fully control are your actions and attitude! Some quick examples are:

- Getting up ten minutes earlier (Win)

- Reading for those ten minutes (Win)

- Setting out your clothes the night before, so they are ready for you (Win)

- Eating a healthy breakfast (Win)

- Leaving for work five minutes earlier, so you are not in as much of a rush (Win)

- Listening to positive or motivational music or a podcast in the car (Win)

That's six wins before you even pull into the parking lot at work!

Now compare that to the alternative of getting up late and not working your brain when you consume nonsense. Or being frustrated because you can't find socks that match, which made you later than you wanted to be, so you had to pick up fast food on the way to work.

Then your body feels like crap, and your mind is foggy—all because you fueled yourself with garbage (the downfalls of which we will cover later in this book). And you are late to your first meeting of the day and anxious because you were not able to prepare appropriately like you wanted to. In reality, you likely also needed to get to work early since you didn't prepare ahead of time as you should have. The worst part of it all? This all went down while listening to negative bullshit or angry music on the car radio.

Can you see how much different your mindset and perspective will be first thing in the morning when you simply get up ten minutes earlier with a plan? The entire list I outlined above that you have control of and that leads to starting the day with a positive mindset happened before you even started your daily list of tasks you needed to do to reach your ultimate short and long-term goals. Which morning routine do you think would produce better results?

Drewbie Wilson, a good friend of mine who I met through Apex, has a saying: "Crush the day before the day crushes you!" Trust me. The day is coming for you, and if you start on the wrong foot, you will be off-balance all day. Nothing will get done with any type of efficiency or quality. You will be so distracted by not being able to collect your thoughts or complete a single task that you won't even realize you had a shit day until your head hits the pillow that night. Then you'll have that gut-wrenching, take-your-breath-away thought of what you forgot to do! That shit is the worst!

For me, the discomfort of getting up early to knock out a quality morning routine is a lot less painful than enduring an entire day where I didn't feel ready to go!

And I love starting every day I possibly can with a win—that's the definition of winning fast and often!

HOW TO WIN FAST AND WIN OFTEN

Everyone's life and situations are different, but having a stable routine is critical to winning fast and often. These are some of my best practices that may help you implement better habits:

- Setting out my gym clothes and clothes for the day the night before.

- Getting up at 4:30 a.m. to exercise and educate myself (I go to the gym at 5:00 a.m. and read from 6-6:30 a.m. typically).

- Coming home, eating, and organizing for the day.

- Using time blocking throughout my week to plan properly.

- Using a task manager for my daily activities that I need to do to maintain my goals.

- Spending time every Sunday to food prep for the week.

- Spending time every Sunday to look at my week, plan out my tasks for each day, and account for contingency planning for surprises that may get in the way of the plan.

There is no one-size-fits-all in planning to win, but what I've shared is a solid foundation to base your strategy on.

The last thing you need to do to ensure success is explain your plan to your ecosystem.

Get your family, leaders, employees, and friends on board with what you are trying to do so they know when and why you are focused on new objectives or changing your priority list. You will likely get some pushback on why you are pivoting and will probably lose some relationships. I struggled through that part of the process. But there is not a single person who has had any level of success that I've spoken to who hasn't lost friends or close relationships during their come up. It is not easy or fun, but I want you to know it's coming so you can prepare yourself.

Your ability to win and reach your goals while feeling like you are winning requires you to create a clear vision for what YOU want, not what you believe OTHERS think you should be doing. I know I said this before, but it is critically important to get it into your head. This won't be the last time I say it, either.

Once you do develop a clear vision, you can then create a plan and process to get to where you want to go. As a bonus, outlining what you need to do and holding yourself accountable for the daily activities necessary to have a successful and productive day will make you feel like a winner and give you a boatload of confidence!

Over the years, I have learned through trial and error what works to reach my goals. I challenge you to make a similar plan to win, to analyze how it goes, and to adjust where you need to ensure you can and will reach your destination.

As this chapter comes to a close, here's an important takeaway: don't give up when it gets tough. The most significant success comes after the biggest struggle —and only when you commit to yourself that you can do it for yourself for all the right reasons!

CHAPTER 4

WINNING MATTERS MORE THAN YOU REALIZE

Competing at the highest level is not about winning.
It's about preparation, courage, understanding,
and nurturing your people and heart.
Winning is the result.
—*Joe Torre*

Several years ago, when Herm Edwards was the coach of the New York Jets, I was watching an interview with him. If I remember correctly, one of the reporters asked Herm, "Did you think that play was going to work?"

Anyone who has seen Herm speak can picture the look on his face when he heard that question. Herm has a unique way of calling you an idiot using nothing more than his facial expressions. It's one of those head-cocked, eyebrows-up, shoulders-dropped gestures that says, "Are you serious!?!" All while burning a hole through the reporter's face.

Herm's response stuck with me for a while because of how simple yet powerful it was. He boiled down exactly what we all need to do when strategizing decision-making. After composing himself so as not to go off on that reporter, he looked right at him and said, "No one in the NFL ever calls a play and thinks, *this one will never work*! We strategize the best we can and call the best plays we can, based on what we know. We implement plays, see how things unfold, and make adjustments as necessary."

I am paraphrasing based on the lesson I took from it—but you get the gist.

TAKING YOUR BEST SHOT

After hearing Herm speak, I was and am very confident that if the play hadn't worked, the players and coaches would have analyzed it to see what went wrong and why it didn't work. Then they would have either made adjustments or retired the play forever. They wouldn't keep using the same plays over and over again and expect different results—especially if they didn't work. That is, by definition, insanity.

The moral of this story is that you should not expect to be perfect. No one is! You make the best decisions you can based on the information you have and what will give you the best chance to accomplish the goal. Herm used his years of experience, film study, player profiles, and personnel skillsets to determine his play-calling and game strategy. He used his assets and tools to guide his team to the ultimate goal of winning while following the game plan that gave him the best chance to win.

You take what you have learned, experienced, and believe to be true and go out in the world and win!

COURSE CORRECT

But how do you adjust when it doesn't feel like you are winning anymore?

How do you know your game plan is aligned to help you win?

How do you course correct when you think you are heading in the wrong direction?

Well, it's Herm to the rescue again.

Another quote of Herm's that stuck with me is, "The greatest thing about sports is you play to win. You don't just play to play. That is what is so great about sports. You play to win. I don't care if you don't have any wins; you go play to win. When you start telling me, it doesn't matter, just retire, and get out, 'cause it matters!"

I can totally relate to this quote as it pertains to playing sports as a kid and even today in my career.

When winning doesn't matter to you anymore, it's a good sign that it's time to move on. It's time to pivot or even start over on a new path. When you feel this way, it might be because you realize that what you are doing isn't what you want to be doing, or you are doing it for the wrong reasons.

Hopefully, based on the last chapter, you know what victory looks like to you now. You know what your end goal is and what daily steps and activities are necessary to get you there. Hopefully, you have a plan you are implementing to create a new routine in your life!

I am sure you have the best intentions to create that new plan and sustain it until you win, but let's be honest, that is not reality. In general, humans struggle with self-control. Many adults find the freedom to do what they want when what they want to do is exciting, but at some point, when plans go a little sideways, they also realize they are responsible for their decisions. In other words, when the shit hits the fan, they have no one to blame but themselves.

The dichotomy of excitement and fear happens regularly with new business owners. You realize every decision is on your shoulders, big or small, and any mistake can cost you the game.

But just like sports, business and life are games of inches.

One play or even one decision can define an entire season!

The challenge of being solely responsible for every decision is scary, and this is why many never own the responsibility of their choices. That is why many people simply float through life, surviving the day instead of winning it. I am sure you are not one of those people, but we all know them. I'm talking about the father who plays more video games than his kids. The woman who spends more time buying workout clothes than doing anything physical in them. The coworker who can't get out of bed on time, who shows up late and does just enough to stay under the radar to keep their job. You don't want to be that type of person, or you wouldn't have invested in yourself by reading this book.

Course correcting involves doing the work and sticking to your plan. If you fall off the wagon, don't throw all your progress away and give up. Get back on that wagon and hang on as best you can as you work your plan.

WHAT THE TOP PERFORMERS PRACTICE

What separates the top performers of the world from the people who just get by?

Top performers spend a lot of time focusing on their best skillsets and attributes. And while this is a smart move, it is also essential to know your weaknesses. Being objective and self-aware allows you to strategize around your weaknesses so you are not held back because of them.

Another bonus of being self-aware? You will be incredibly powerful in creating a game plan to capitalize on strengths while avoiding weaknesses! I am sure you have heard Henry Ford's quote, "If you think you can, or you think you can't, you are right." I take that to mean the ability to be self-aware and focus on what your strengths are while avoiding your weaknesses helps you move through life with fewer obstacles.

Imagine putting all your efforts and focus on what you are best at every day for 90 days, 180 days, or 24 months. Imagine how much better your life would be than grinding through sludge every day doing something you are not meant to do.

Another amazing benefit of being self-aware is that it allows you to better understand and have empathy for others. Knowing how and why you think the way you do allows you to put yourself in other people's shoes. When you do this, you use the same perspective that allows you to better understand where they are coming from and why they are the way they are. We have all experienced situations where we just cannot understand why someone is feeling the way they are or acting the way they are. You listen to how they are feeling and then tell yourself that they just don't make any sense.

The better your self-awareness, the better your environmental awareness, which makes it easier to handle situations and guide them to a resolution. You can do this because you have learned how to take your ego out of the equation and insert empathy instead!

Being self-aware is a start, but I also know one of the most underutilized attributes in underperforming people is discipline. Motivation comes and goes, but high-performing people who stay disciplined to their game plan (especially when they don't feel like it) become champions.

If you are struggling with choosing a habit that will move you forward, you can do something about that tomorrow morning. It's as simple as waking up and starting your day with the task you least want to do.

But before you can figure out what you don't want to do, you have to figure out everything you have to do.

First, prioritize what you need to do every day, then create a routine that kicks off the day with the thing you want to do the least. You will need to have a strong guiding force to remind yourself of why you need to stay dedicated when every cell in your body wants to stay in bed or avoid the necessary tasks!

I firmly believe that we all need to create an image in our brain of the person who represents the voice in the back of our head. You know, the voice that says, "GET UP AND GET TO WORK." My image is my future self. I am typically a pretty good motivator, but like anyone else, at certain times, I just don't feel like doing the hard stuff. So, I picture myself coaching someone else and what I would do or say if one of my clients gave me my bullshit excuse. The future me is an amazing business coach who constantly reminds me why I do what I do. If I can't coach myself well, I surely can't coach others well.

So, that is typically where my mind goes when I need a kick in the ass. It might sound egotistical, but it works for me.

**It's funny; I am the best coach for me,
just like I am also the worst critic of myself.**

CORE VALUES

That character in the back of your head (just like my future coach that I mentioned), speaking the voice that you hear, good or bad, is built from a set of core values. These values are used to lead your life, business, and family.

I am sure you have heard of core values before and hopefully have some you have thought of as well. But do you live by them every day, in every decision? Do they align with your vision of success and where you want to be? Have you written them out to read daily so you can hold yourself accountable?

Just like my son asks, "How strong?" and knows, "Too Strong!" is the only answer, you need to be self-aware enough to coach yourself through the times when you are not motivated or excited. If you do not believe you are reliable enough, pick someone you believe in but who also sees you as a person they can believe in.

People who take ownership of their decisions and focus on what they can do to better themselves win a lot more often than those who have no guiding force.

I was one of the people just floating by for a long time. I spent years of my life at 300-plus pounds. I just went with the flow, with nothing motivating me to do much of anything outside of what I wanted to do at the moment to soothe my immediate desires. I would eat whatever I wanted or what was most convenient. I would drink whatever I wanted or what was most convenient. I hung out with whomever I wanted and slept with whomever I wanted or who was most convenient. It was not a proud season of my life, but it wasn't until I got a clear vision of what I wanted, why I wanted it, and what my core values were that I could course correct.

Then it was time for me to take ownership of what my life was going to be. It was time to want to win again. I was ready to retire that season of my life and make decisions for a reason instead of convenience.

Below is a list of the core values that I identified and that I work to live by every day today:

Communicate Proactively

- Set proper expectations
- Plan ahead so problems can be solved proactively when expectations change
- Take ownership and accountability of one's own task

Operate with a Help First Mentality

- Uncover and solve problems as the top priority
- A no-sales sales approach
- Look for opportunities to add value
- Give without expectations

Appreciate Everyone's Time

- Remain timely with deliverables
- Early is on time
- Be prepared
- Respect your own time

Continually Evolve

- Have a growth mindset
- Continued self-education
- Test and try new things
- Fail forward

Have a Championship Mindset

- Play to the whistle
- Be blissfully dissatisfied
- Play the long game
- Do the work others won't

Still, I am far from perfect. But when I analyze the decisions I need to make or have made, I compare them to these priorities in my life. I have control over my core values. If I try to do anything else, I lose control. I forget the rudder guiding my ship. Most importantly, even if I get a little off course, I don't stop working.

Like many driven people, just because I am not as disciplined in a moment, it does not mean I have stopped moving. But unfortunately, when you don't have the proper guiding force, you will end up somewhere you did not expect to. This means even when you are hustling, if you are not strongly connected to your core values, you can look up hours, days, or weeks later and have no idea how you got so far off track.

I didn't end up 300-plus pounds with a drinking problem and bad depression without effort. My effort had no guidance. I have to be the best at everything I do and trust me; I could drink more, eat more, and lift more than pretty much anyone I knew. I was a champion at making shitty decisions.

Vision and core values are the only tools you need to adjust yourself when the tides change, when the storms hit, and when it becomes too dark to see your way out!

But before you can use your rudder, you have to define how to create that rudder. That is how you will create the guidance you need.

To get started, first, create a list of core values you want to use as the rudder of your ship. These are what will guide you when you are getting off track. Start with the three to five things that you use to hold yourself accountable, then add to the list. This can be a living document until you feel it is fully accurate, but don't change it regularly.

If you don't know how to create your core values, look around your life and find people you view as successful. Ask them what they use to hold themselves accountable. Find out what core values drive their decisions or keep them disciplined. Make sure to talk to people who represent the life and achievements you want. Be careful with who you ask, but be open to asking several people in different aspects of your life and combining their core values as your own. Implementing the best practices of people you respect will help you pivot and see a different perspective. Like Herm says, "If winning isn't important to you, get out because winning matters!"

The biggest thing to understand when creating the vision you want is to identify the daily tasks to get you there and the core values to keep you on the right path, so you can't lie to yourself. You can fool many others through what you do and say, but when you lie down at night, you are alone with the inner judge and jury. And if you are lying to yourself, you will lose to that internal judge every time. When you break a commitment to yourself, you start to lose trust and confidence in yourself. You put your life in the hands of short-term self-satisfying things that hurt you and those around you. If someone else lets you down repeatedly, you might lose faith in them or cut them out of your life altogether. Unfortunately, you are stuck with yourself, so losing confidence in your decision-making is the only result when you lie to yourself.

This leads you down a dangerous path.

JUSTIFYING SHITTY BEHAVIOR

Once your confidence is gone, you listen to the voices in your head that tell you how you "deserve" the things you want even though you're off course. This simply justifies your inherent lack of effort and discipline.

Does any of this sound familiar?

- "I had a good week at work, so I deserve a few drinks."
- "I ate right this week, so I deserve pizza and ice cream."
- "I worked hard this month, so I deserve a vacation."

TRICKLE-DOWN EFFECT

We only have to soothe our internal demons when we have not accomplished what we set out to do. Otherwise, those demons—like guilt—are quiet. We don't have to pay attention to them. They aren't loud. Soothing our demons and caving into doing what's bad for us destroys progress. It ruins your relationship with yourself, which can have a trickle-down effect on your entire life. Your job or company will suffer, your spouse and kids will suffer, even your friends will suffer.

Not to blow your poor decisions out of proportion, but they can affect generations of your family because of how your kids see you acting. The environment you are creating at home impacts far more than just you. And you know you are way #TooStrong to let your great-grandkids suffer because you couldn't get your shit together.

In the world of social media influencers, it does not take many followers to be considered an influencer. At home, you influence your family; online, you influence your followers. What type of impact are you putting out into the world? Does it match the impact you are getting back? How are you influencing your trickle-down effect?

Business owners, for example, carry the responsibility of many people. You can have a positive and negative impact on every employee's family member based on how you show up to work every day, how you structure your time, and how you approach problems.

Ultimately how you communicate both verbally and non-verbally has a massive impact on the world around you. And this will be a negative consequence — all because you allowed yourself to divert from the plan you told yourself you needed to stick to so you could be successful in YOUR EYES. Remember, you are #TooStrong to give up on your dreams. You are #TooStrong to let yourself down!

Have you ever been around or seen a person who is angry all the time, but no one knows why they are this way? It is very likely because they have let themselves down. The angriest people I have met are that way because of commitments they have broken to themselves. Their gap in accomplishment leads to them feeling empty and lost because they are so off track from where they wanted to be. Now, not only are they not winning anymore, but they also are not playing the game they initially set out to play!

They become frustrated, jealous, and vindictive because they hate those who have the self-control to chase their priorities.

A well-known saying by Mark Twain perfectly fits this scenario: "Never argue with stupid people. They will drag you down to their level and beat you with experience."

The same is true when engaging with those who struggle with discipline. People like that use the same excuses on you that they used on themselves when they strayed from their path.

You've heard these excuses before. But here are a handful to make sure we are on the same page:

- "Why are you working so hard?"

- "Maybe you should slow down?"

- "Dude, it's one drink!"

People who have broken promises to themselves talk to other people in that manner unknowingly much of the time. That's because when you stay disciplined (and the disgruntled people see this), it shines a light on all the reasons and excuses they have given themselves about why winning doesn't matter anymore. It shines a light on their lies. But what you do matters, so you need to stay focused on owning your decisions and being driven by the right guiding forces instead of the people around you who want to force you to justify your bad decisions to make themselves feel better about their downfalls.

In the next chapter, I am going to cover ways to fuel yourself for the battle of winning against the influences of a mediocre world. And you better read up! It's one of the most important chapters in the book because there are a lot of people out there who would be more than happy to pull you off the track.

If you are struggling with communication and finding your guiding core values, check out my YouTube Channel: *Mike Claudio*. You'll find a ton of videos to help you. Make sure you subscribe and leave a comment on the video that helped you the most!

CHAPTER 5

FUELING YOUR MACHINE

Take care of your body.
It's the only place you have to live.
—Jim Rohn

Emotion drives action.

That's not an opinion; it's a scientific fact.

It is how humans decide what will make them happy or sad.

Emotion drives people toward what is right and moves them away from what's wrong and dangerous.

As I mentioned earlier, it is what the best sales and marketing companies use to win us over.

If emotion drives action, then how we feel provokes our reaction and physically drives how we see and respond to everything. In turn, how we feel controls how quickly we can focus on and make decisions. That feeling will either push us to do one more rep at the gym or eat one more cookie on the couch.

This chapter is for you if you are not satisfied with your current situation.

If you love your body, yourself, and everything in your life, please don't change anything! Then feel free to skip ahead to the next chapter.

Many people relate the opinions of others to what they are currently doing. I know this because I follow successful people, and sometimes it makes me question what I do. Yes, it's wise to audit yourself, but if you are generally happy, please take this chapter for what it is. It may help you if you need it, but you may not need many or any of the points I cover here.

This chapter is a breakdown of my opinion and approach to staying physically and mentally fit so I can perform at the highest level possible. If you are looking to improve, please implement what makes sense to you, but if you are happy, don't let me or anyone else change what's working for you.

Maybe some of what I am sharing will help you make tweaks to your routine so you can win more. That's great, but I also want to encourage you to own your happiness, to be self-aware, to determine if you are thrilled about how your health and fitness are going. If your response to this question is automatic, meaning you say you are happy, but you don't really feel it and know you are letting yourself down, then read this chapter and implement my advice. It helped me, and it can help you, too.

A lot of people will push you to love yourself for who you are, and that is great if you genuinely believe it and if you feel good about yourself. But if you are trying to convince yourself to be happy with what you see in the mirror and feel in your heart, so you don't have to face the facts of how you truly feel, then you are not doing everything you can to be the best you. If this sounds like you, it's time to start being real and making changes in your life, one decision at a time!

YOU ARE A MACHINE

What we consume and how we fuel our bodies drives our emotional state. How you think and perform is directly related to what you feed the machine. Are you pumping unleaded or jet fuel into your body?

As I mentioned earlier, I spent a good part of my early twenties weighing over 300 pounds. Right now, I am sitting at around 240 pounds of twisted steel and sex appeal. Not precisely, but compared to how big I was, I am so much happier with how I look and feel. It was not a quick and easy trip to the top of the weight class, and it was a battle through the valley of death on the way back. What worked and didn't work for me didn't matter because I had a mission and vision for what I wanted and why. I'll share a little more about my story before I jump into the physical and emotional health practices that help me Win Fast and Win Often.

MY YOUNG ADULT COME UP

After I failed out of college, I was in a bad spot.

I went from smoking a pack of cigarettes a day and drinking a case of beer three or four times a week to cold turkey everything.

The morning of the final exam of my freshman year, I woke up in an empty dorm room thinking, *what the fuck just happened?* I realized I had been a passenger in my life for the last 12 to 18 months, and it scared me straight. I don't want to call it an awakening, but when I woke up, I had clarity on the fact that I had done jack shit for over a year. My dorm room was packed up and empty, and I discovered that my college career was over, baseball was over, and my life appeared to be over. I had just taken the biggest loss of my life and had to drive home with a metaphorical giant black eye and my tail between my legs. I was about to face my parents and admit complete and total failure. That prospect is what literally scared me sober.

I went into that exam and failed it. Then I drove home and never looked back. I hated the person I had become and knew I had to make wild changes in my life.

I stopped drinking and quit smoking that day.

It has now been over 15 years since I've had a cigarette, and I spent the two years after failing out of college not having a drink. I went through some rough times in the first few weeks after I quit, feeling like a failure living at home as I dealt with the withdrawals of cutting off everything cold turkey. Now, I know that not going back to that school environment was one of the best decisions I ever made for myself.

Talk about choosing me regardless of what people around me wanted to do!

My entire family has college and graduate degrees under their belts, and I am the one who couldn't pass freshman year. As you can imagine, my decision not to go back didn't go over well with my parents. I can't explain why, but I just knew college was not the right place for me. And I was surer about not going back than any decision I had made in the previous years—I had to stick to it for me.

I will never forget the day I told my dad, "Going back to school's a waste of your money and my time. It's not for me."

I remember standing at the top of the driveway, talking to my dad about not going back. He had his typical concerned/frustrated expression and patented double-eyebrow stance. Head slightly tilted back, eyebrows scrunched together and down toward his nose: this was his death stare. It said to me, "I don't know what you are about to say, but I don't think I am going to like it!" I stood there, searching for the words to tell him about my decision while being scared to death of following my gut and letting him down. Of letting down the family name. I mean, for God's sake, my grandfather came to America with no education, and he put four kids through college. But I couldn't even make it past freshman year? How was that a great way for me to pay him back for his sacrifice? How could I represent the Claudio name around town as the kid who couldn't cut it? What would happen when I would see all my friends' parents and know they would think, *I wonder why he couldn't cut it?* Or, *What a waste of a talented young man.* My biggest fear was that people would judge my parents because of my decision.

My parents were both well-connected in the community, and I still had brothers in high school, so they would also see a lot of these mutual parents of friends. To be honest, I was more afraid of how my dropping out would impact my family than of how it would affect my future.

Maybe it was God, or maybe it was blind testosterone, but I knew deep down that I could be successful without college. I also knew that if I went back to that same college, I would fall so much farther into that deep dark hole that it wouldn't matter what degree I got. If I followed that path, I would be too broken to use any of what I learned.

Ultimately, I ignored the 100 reasons to go back and stuck to the one reason that mattered the most to me. I knew going back to school was a waste of my time and my father's money because it was not where I belonged. In my heart, going back was the wrong decision, and yes, it was not what my mom or dad wanted to hear, but I still had to follow through on what was best for me.

My parents grew up in a time where if you didn't go to college, you would end up a bum. So, it took a while for the three of us to see eye to eye on my choice. My dad and I fought about it a lot over the course of a few years. To complicate matters, all my friends were still in college.

It wasn't until my youngest brother graduated college with a master's degree and struggled to find a job he loved or that paid what he wanted it to that my dad could see maybe I hadn't made the worst decision ever.

Internally, my lack of college education was the chip on my shoulder that I needed to push through and make my goals happen no matter what.

I told myself when I was 18 that I was not going to let the lack of a college degree be my defining moment. It was the first time I looked at what at the time was perceived as a loss and decided it was not going to keep me down or hold me back. Then I went so far as to take the money I was making at my first job to buy a house when I was just 19 years old. I wanted to prove that I could be successful without that piece of paper everyone was so rabidly chasing.

As I reflect back on purchasing that townhouse at such a young age, I can see what came about from that purchase—it was a valuable lesson in parenting and unconditional love.

I can't remember why but right before I bought the townhouse, I knew I didn't want to waste money on rent. My thought was, *I am making good money, so why would I want to hand it to someone else?*

Shortly after that, I found a new townhouse community in the early stages of construction, and I thought I could get a pretty good deal on one. So, I asked my dad if he would cosign a mortgage for me. Pretty ballsy, huh? Asking the man who I thought viewed me as a failure and embarrassment to put his credit on the line so I could buy a townhouse. Yes, I was that guy. To this day, I don't know what he saw in me that gave him any faith that I would be able to support that level of responsibility, but to his credit, he helped me take a very important step in life.

I made it my mission to never have to ask him to help me make a single bill or mortgage payment, and I was successful. I will say you learn a lot and grow up really fast when you're a kid and waste so much money on bullshit that you are not sure you'll be able to make your next mortgage payment.

That said, I believe that not going back to college was the most mature and responsible decision I had made in my short 19 years of life! I wish it had been the lowest point I had to go through to get to where I am today, but there are plenty of lows in my journey.

Still, I learned so many valuable lessons from climbing back from rock bottom, the worst of which I shared at the beginning of this book. I learned how to keep myself mentally focused and my emotions under control. I also had to become so much more self-aware and comfortable with who I am. That all stemmed from how I fueled myself to enable my greatest potential to make the best decisions.

Think about the last time you had a hell of a Saturday night. You probably went out and drank too much, ate unhealthy food, stayed up late, and then slept late. You might have hung out with negative people. Maybe you spent most of the night talking shit about the world, the country, people, and celebrities. That is as much junk food for your brain as fast food is for your body (and brain!)

If you are over the age of 25 and pulled a night like that on the weekend, likely, you did not feel like yourself again until Wednesday of the next week! You missed days of feeling as sharp as you could, skipped the gym, and didn't stop eating quick and easy junk food because you didn't feel like cooking or buying healthier food. This is an example of your body and mind giving you what you give it. Put crap into your body, and it will give you crap back.

Staying healthy consists of physical and mental health.

It requires exercise, diet, mediation, and spiritual connection. One is not more important than the other, but if you want to win, you have to focus on all aspects that keep you healthy.

Nothing will make you prouder than realizing you are #TooStrong to succumb to the bullshit excuses of the world that will keep you average. Greatness does not come easy.

Naturally, that includes the paces you need to put your body through.

EXERCISE

Creating consistency around exercise is the hardest obstacle when you start a routine. But it's far easier to maintain your health and habits once you get your routine going. Getting your blood flowing every day is excellent for your mind and body. It helps wake you up and get you ready for the day. If you have not been working out, once you begin, it is going to hurt. You are going to be sore but remember that will pass.

It was around the third or fourth time when I ripped through the back seam of my pants that I decided I didn't want to be 300 pounds anymore. I knew I had to make a change. I had gotten into powerlifting and competitive eating after college. And when I went downhill, I was only competing with myself on how much more shit I could consume that day versus the day before.

It was ugly.

I knew I had to do something, and I did.

At the time, I could bench press 450 pounds, but I could not reach the back of my head. I literally could not reach my hand to the back of my head or across my body to my shoulder. Pick your hand up and scratch the back of your head and rub your left shoulder. I couldn't do that without putting my elbow on a wall and leaning into it. If you had told me that would be a chunk of my life, I wouldn't have believed you. It's crazy that I had fallen so far. My wife met me around this time, and she can tell you the reality. Putting my collar down on a dress shirt was a team sport. I couldn't wrap my arms around myself, and I would have to loop my belt through my pants *before* I put them on. I needed to perch my elbow on the shower wall and turn toward it to wash my shoulder. Putting shoes on was a multi-step process because I could not breathe when I bent over. Shit was hard, and I hated myself for it.

Many of the things I take for granted now I struggled with then. I laugh about it in retrospect because of how incredibly stupid I must have looked just getting in and out of a car, trying to get dressed, or simply walking up or down the stairs. It was sad how far out of shape I had gotten and how negatively it impacted my mood, thoughts, and mindset. The only reason I can laugh now is that I beat my health issues. I overcame them and now can see what it takes to conquer so much more in my life.

It wasn't comfortable getting to such a heavy weight, and it wasn't easy getting back. But you have to start doing something when it's time to change your game. You have to set the right expectations for yourself and then simply start.

I started with the elliptical. Twenty minutes a day. You would have thought I was running a marathon. What kept me going was an accountability partner. Having a person to hold you accountable and who will pat you on the back or kick you in the ass when you need it is huge when you are carving out a new routine. That's because it is easier for many of us to commit to not letting others down than it is to commit to not letting ourselves down. My friend, Lauren, who worked at the YMCA, was my accountability partner. We had gone to high school together, and she could see I needed the extra push. I happened to be doing my cardio exercises around the same time she was there, so we started working out next to each other. She was honestly the only reason I kept up with it. Then I took accountability to the extreme a few months later when a buddy of mine invited me to his CrossFit Gym. Little did I know how that would turn out for me. Let's just say the power of group training is incredible.

When I moved to Charlotte, I started at one CrossFit gym but then moved to another. You have to find a group of people you can relate to and who push you, and I needed to do a little looking around before I landed at the right gym. When you continue to challenge yourself through group classes and challenging workouts, joining a CrossFit gym can change you as a person.

My wife and I settled at CrossFit Weddington because Coach Cory and the culture he creates as the owner of the gym is so collaborative. There is something about suffering alongside someone who builds amazing friendships and who drives you to show up every day and be 1% better than yesterday. That is why running groups and road bike groups work so well. Humans want to be part of a community of like-minded people. CrossFit keeps that team atmosphere and competitive focus that I need. However, you need to find your community of people, even if it is just a group of men or women in your neighborhood who go for a walk four times a week.

The consequences of deciding to work out consistently were incredible. I was around people with a greater drive to do more and who relied on their positive thinking, which modeled for me a different way of regularly doing life. When you are around the right people, you will have more positive conversations and hear more about people's successes in and out of the gym. These conversations were night and day compared to the ones I'd had at the bar or at work with friends and coworkers who didn't have the same outlook on life.

Spend time with the right types of people, and you will also pile up daily wins, which create the winning streak we talked about earlier. You will begin to look better, too, which boosts your confidence. Looking good is the first step to feeling good. When you feel more confident, you will do things you never thought you could do, which increases a belief in yourself in other aspects of your life.

After that first pull-up or muscle-up, you will feel like you can accomplish anything—maybe even your first half-marathon or 10K. Go that far, and you will surprise and impress yourself even more with what you are capable of. Then you will look for even more places to find that same feeling. Maybe it will be at work or with your family. The confidence born from exercise and doing things you never thought you could do will fill your life with something you never thought you would have—the mindset of "I can do anything I put my mind to!" This will change your life forever. Suddenly, "impossible" becomes "accomplishment." A thought of, *is it possible*, changes to, *what daily steps do I need to take to get there to make it a reality?*

But if you are not healthy, everything in life will be more difficult. You won't feel like you can win.

In that situation, you will continue to focus on what you can't do, and that will only bring more losses than wins to your life. So, focus on one decision at a time and get yourself exercising consistently to beat that feeling. It doesn't need to be CrossFit seven days a week. But get moving and sweat five days a week every week. Before long, you will find excuses *to* work out because of how it makes you feel instead of searching for reasons *not to* work out. Holding yourself accountable for daily exercise is in your control and can help you create regular wins in your life. So, get up and get going today! If you have been working out but are just going through the motions, try something else that will get you excited and keep you coming back.

If you need inspiration to find a program that works, check out the 75 Hard program created by Andy Frisella. This is not an exercise program, but it will hold you accountable for changing your life. If you look it up and decide to do it, shoot me a DM on Instagram: @winrateconsulting. I completed it in 2019, and it changed my life 100%. I would love to help you through it.

DIET

When I started my journey back to nutrition, I had no idea there were so many diet plans out there. To be clear, I am not a physician or dietitian, but I have tried all these diet plans and feel like I can speak on my experience with them. I have done keto, Paleo, Whole30, gluten-free, dairy-free, flexible dieting, macro counting, and intermittent fasting. As I stated previously, I win because I don't give up, not because I have never failed. You will fail at finding a diet plan that works, too, when you are learning what nutrition plans are effective for you, but don't let that stop you.

The biggest misconception I have seen when it comes to fueling yourself is that changes happen quickly. But remember, you didn't gain weight overnight, and you won't lose it that way either. So many people try a new diet plan for a week or two and quit when they don't see results. When it comes to fueling your body, you have to take it one decision and one meal at a time. If you get off track or lose self-control and discipline at a meal, don't throw away the rest of the day or weekend. When you don't eat right, you will feel sluggish and tired. You will be plagued by the mental fog that limits your decision-making capabilities and puts you in a depressed state. We've all had a big burger and fries for lunch and then felt like ass for the rest of the day. You know that feeling of being tired, sluggish, and agitated. If you do this every day, you are operating at 50% capacity or less half the time. How do you expect to win if you can't even think straight and work effectively?

You can't.

When you fall off the nutrition wagon or get out of your routine, analyze why your plan didn't work and adjust. Then get back to your mission as soon as you can, using the rudder we created in the last chapter to get you going in the right direction once more. If you are feeling discouraged, remember, the only failure in eating healthy and dieting is giving up. Everything else is a constant work in progress!

I wanted each of the diets I tried to be a staple in my life, but when they didn't work, I refused to give up on my goal of being healthier. So many people in the health and wellness world want you to believe you can take a pill or complete a 30-day routine to be ready for beach season. That shit is fake and a lie. It's on the level with people who say you can make a million dollars a month with an online dropship company. It takes a lot more time, effort, wins, and losses to make these goals happen.

I have proven this over time.

It is only possible to win when you refuse to give up and keep trying new systems until you find one that works for you. And here's a secret, this approach works for anything you want to accomplish—not just dieting. If you want to win in any aspect of life, keep working at it, and don't stop searching for the right plan until you find it.

Eating the right food is different for everyone, but you need to fuel optimally to perform optimally in the gym, board room, and everywhere in between. You can't walk into a meeting "hangry" and expect to accomplish anything productive. Even when I decided to lose weight, I was not going to let a diet that didn't work stop me.

Once you have decided you are sick and tired of being sick and tired, the change in your life happens one decision at a time. The best decision I made to help me stick to my daily decisions that I knew would pay off and make my nutrition plan easier was instituting food/meal prep. I do this on Sunday, but you can pick whatever day works for you. Spending a few hours cooking and preparing food for the week will change your eating regimen permanently. It is hard to find healthy food on the fly, so you need to be proactive. If you're not, you will pay out more money than if you just made meals and snacks yourself, and you will likely not make good eating decisions because you will choose to eat from a place of desperation. Just like everything else, make a plan and stick to it, one decision at a time. If you look at your plan as one meal or even one bite at a time, it is a lot easier than thinking of what it will take to lose 25 or 50 pounds.

Don't forget: you are attacking this goal in the same way you are attacking every goal outlined earlier in the book. You are grinding your goals down into manageable and easy-to-control pieces. When you take it one bite at a time, your ability to function changes.

The goal of dieting well is to reduce inflammation. When you eat bad food or drink alcohol, your body holds water or swells a little. Having more inflammation in your body affects your ability to think, make decisions quickly, and react in a timely manner. All of that hurts your ability to perform at your best. I didn't realize how poorly I was operating until I focused on eating clean, not drinking, and hydrating properly. You will be amazed at the changes you will feel. It's the same as being in the gym, where you learn what you are capable of when you focus on fueling your body correctly.

One of the most undervalued actions that help you take care of your body well is proper hydration. I thought I drank enough water until I figured out that I needed at least a gallon a day to keep my body where it needed to be.

An increase in my mental clarity and a lack of soreness is the biggest tell-tale sign that I am hydrated. I can also tell when I haven't drunk enough water in a day because I have trouble making decisions quickly or at all, and my body aches a little. Overall, being hydrated helps you sleep better, and it curbs your appetite. And many times, even when you feel hungry, you are not. That feeling you interpret as hunger is your body telling you to hydrate. So, the next time you are hungry and between the main meals of the day, drink 20 to 30 ounces of water and see if you still are.

Being successfully hydrated requires you to plan and have a water bottle with you regularly. It is essential that you drink water as well because all the artificial drinks on the market do nothing for you except mess with your system. Water is what you need.

Brain Fuel

Right after I left corporate America to work for a small construction company, I dove headfirst into the entrepreneurship world. I wanted to learn more about the new and wild environment I was in without the comfort of a big corporation protecting me. If you are in the corporate space, don't kid yourself. Your superiors tell you just enough so you can do your job, and they pay you just enough, too, so you won't ask too many questions.

Once I made the leap out from under the protection of the corporate umbrella, I realized I was incredibly uneducated on more than selling technology. I knew there would be a learning curve, but was I ever blown away at how much there was to learn.

What surprised me the most was figuring out that the majority of what I needed to learn did not need to come from a class or textbook. I needed to learn the life lessons of those who had been through similar things.

Now I realize the power of having a business coach since it is what I do for a living, but when I was getting started, I had no idea where or how to find the information I needed to be successful in my new world of decision-making. So, I just started asking around.

> **You would be amazed at how many people in the
> entrepreneurship space are not only
> willing to provide guidance but love doing it.**

People who have struggled to get to where they are (and who have done it the right way) love helping newcomer entrepreneurs avoid the same shortfalls that tripped them up early in their game.

I was always good at asking for advice and feedback from upper management at Verizon, so I just went with what I knew and started asking people who appeared to be smarter or more successful than me what and how they did what they did. I also realized a lot of those people had gone through the phase I was in. That being the case, many directed me toward the specific people they followed or a book or podcast that had given them valuable information. I started one page and one episode at a time and continued to consume as much information as I could as fast as I could.

When I was digging into podcasts and watching videos while getting into the entrepreneurship world working as the head of sales for very small companies, I noticed a consistent theme. Every successful person interviewed attributed some, if not all, of their success to reading. I was 27 when I thought, *why am I the dumbass not reading?* Seven years of ingesting other people's lessons and advice later, and I have not slowed down in my reading at all.

But when I first made the promise to start reading, I sucked at doing it for several reasons. When I was growing up, I was told I sucked at it, so I believed my parents, teachers, and the specialty learning centers I attended. I don't think anyone had the intent to knock me down. Regardless, I could not remember a damn thing I'd ever read. Another reason I thought I sucked was that I'd been diagnosed with ADD/ADHD, which I now know just means I was too awesome for people to handle (lol)!

Still, those challenges did cause me to struggle with reading comprehension, mostly because my attention span was that of a gnat in a tornado. In this area, like in so many other areas of my life, I listened to everyone else and stopped reading. As a kid, I thought, *if everyone tells me I suck at it, why should I believe any different?* Fortunately, I didn't hold onto that opinion of myself, and like I always do, I made a change because I wasn't happy. Also, like I always do, once I made that change, I went all in.

In 2016, I read six books, and in 2017, I read 15. I had no real plan or strategy for this new venture of mine other than making the commitment to read more when I felt like it or had downtime. Here's a tip: if you feel like you never have downtime, that's a sign you have the time—you just have to make it! I kept going with my reading goal and, in 2018, had a talk with myself about getting real. I told myself that I had to overcome my reading weakness and make it a strength instead. My new goal was to read 52 two books in a year.

I knew if I could read every day, I could make it happen. So, I started out on the best foot I could. I read 30 minutes in the morning and 30 minutes at night, reading two books at a time. In the morning, I would read a book about business to get my mind focused for the day, and at night I would read non-fiction biographies and autobiographies to end my day with a story. I loved reading about how successful people from all periods of life made decisions.

Also, in 2018, my second son Everett was born. That slowed my reading routine down some, but I still completed 45 books. I know what you are thinking: *those must have been short little books, Mike.* Man, I wish. In truth, these books ranged from a couple of hundred pages to the most extensive book that was close to 1,000 pages, *The Rise of Theodore Roosevelt.* That's probably my favorite book of them all. If you want to stop feeling sorry for yourself, read that book, and you will instantly feel grateful for what you have.

As I got better at reading, I looked forward to it. That much I expected because once you make something a priority, it becomes a habit you can't wait to do. You might even feel a little awkward or off when you don't do it. What I was not expecting or prepared for was how my brainpower changed. It wasn't just that I knew more, but I operated more effectively and made decisions more quickly and with more confidence. Because I worked my brain muscle every day, it got stronger. I looked at things more clearly than I had in my life. Working your brain is no different than working your abs. If you put in a little work, you won't look terrible, but until you push yourself, you won't see significant results.

CONTROLLING YOUR MINDSET AND HABITS

That realization led me to audit everything my brain was consuming. *Who or what was I listening to on the radio? Who was I spending time with? When I looked online or at social media, was I following and engaging with the right people?* I reviewed how every decision I made impacted me.

It is easy to get pulled into gossip and negative news stories and follow a train wreck of a person online. But when you do this, it impacts how you view your world. If you are listening to aggressive and angry music, you will be hostile and aggressive. If you look to a conspiracy theorist all the time, you will become a conspiracy theorist. If you listen to your neighbor bitch about her husband, you will bitch about yours. If you hang out with guys who talk about women and go to bars all the time, you will question what you have at home since you aren't doing the same thing.

That's human nature.

Instead of getting sucked into such negativity, I suggest finding a handful of people who you align with consistently. Make sure these people are where you want to be or that they have what you hope to have. That means you should relate to these people and believe in what they say and believe. I used to listen to dozens of people every day who all shared their advice and the way they did business and life. There are so many different opinions and ideas that can lead to success, just like there is no right or wrong way to reach your goals. If you start to listen to too many people or coaches, you can feel conflicted about who to listen to.

My advice is to find a few people you believe in and follow them consistently. I listen to Andy Frisella, Ed Mylett, and Ryan Stewman. I bought into what they have to say because they represent what winning looks like at all times. That is what I want to portray.

I know this is easy for me to say as a business coach, but hiring a coach and getting their outside perspective on how to accomplish what you want to do can be one of the best actions you ever take. Many people have gone through what you haven't prepared for yet. The strength of their experience will shorten your failure gap and help you learn what you need so you can Win Fast and Win Often at everything else you do. I have personally bought into the training programs and masterminds of all three of these men, and not only have I learned a ton but being in their programs put me around many more like-minded people.

I am not telling you to hire me. I am telling you to find a mentor who can help you down your path. The unfortunate truth is that the best ones charge for it. Anyone giving away a bunch of "knowledge" for free and touting that it will make you rich is not real. And if you won't pay for the coaching you need, you need to ask if you believe in yourself enough to invest in yourself. People who don't believe in themselves are tough to coach because they struggle to commit to making it work or actually doing the work. They look for the easiest, fastest, and cheapest way to get what they want. When you break it down, that mindset is a fairytale and not the reality of what it takes. So, make sure you are not that person, find a proven warrior in your line of success, and then consume everything they have to say!

I have always heard that you are the average of the five people you spend the most time around, but it's a hard concept to grasp until you've lived it yourself. It's also hard to grasp how changing who you spend time around can massively influence your brainpower.

YOU'LL LEAVE SOME PEOPLE BEHIND

Now let me say this as we close the chapter. As you try to level up and improve your situation, you will encounter some unforeseen and unfortunate circumstances. You will lose friendships and relationships you did not intend to lose—including friends who have been a huge part of your life and who won't stick around when you say no to going out. I'll be honest, this part of the process sucks. There is no minimizing that. What kept me going was the vision of what I wanted for my family. That was more significant than any single relationship. Yes, you will cut out some bad seeds, and that will help you, but what will hurt the most is losing close people unintentionally.

When you change your priorities and how you are making decisions, many won't understand it. You might hear questions like these:

"Why last week were you willing to drink all night with me, and this week, you want to get to bed earlier?"

"Why last week did you go to the movies, and this week, you want to go to the gym instead?"

"Why last week did you meet us for pizza, and this week, you want to stay in to read or prep food for the week?"

Many people will not understand the sacrifices you have to make in the short term to reach your long-term success. Prepare for this as it happens to everyone who levels up. Some people in your life are comfortable with the level they're at now. There's nothing wrong with that, and you shouldn't look down on them—

just like they shouldn't look down on you for wanting more. But you might not feel the same way and need more. It's okay to go after it even when you feel pain.

The bottom line is that what got you to where you are right now will never get you to where you want to go. This mindset applies to habits, diet, exercise, or relationships. You have to decide how bad you want it. Changes will be necessary and painful, but if you make educated decisions with the bigger picture in mind, over time, you will improve and get one step closer to where you want to be. To fix yourself, you have to adjust how you fuel the machine, and that starts with your next decision and how it will impact every aspect of your life.

CHAPTER 6

LOOK GREAT, FEEL GREAT, PERFORM GREAT

Health is the greatest gift, contentment the greatest wealth, faithfulness the best relationship.
—Buddha

You have seven seconds to make a first impression.

First impressions are as real in person as they are online in this day and age. The average view time of a video on Facebook is ten seconds.[1] That means you have the blink of an eye to grab someone's attention and get them to want more.

I am not talking about good looks. Not everyone has the perfect build or muscle tone, and most people don't have the best wardrobe or own an exotic car. And some people don't have great hair—if they have hair at all. Still, putting more thought into your appearance is one of the easiest ways to improve your self-image, confidence, and the way people see you. It is non-verbal communication that encompasses the way you dress, your grooming, body language, and etiquette. It's not that your social life will be a loss if you don't look perfect, but if you slack off with your appearance, then you're making things harder than they have to be.

Incredibly, the power of appearance affects how you feel and how others feel about you. My mom was always a stickler for looking your best. For the longest time and probably still today, she did not love facial hair on her boys and regularly yelled at me to shave. Now that I've had a beard for years, I think it has started growing on her—or she just gave up!

---

[1] "Facebook Video Statistics," 99 Firms, accessed July 8, 2021, https://99firms.com/blog/facebook-video-statistics/#gref.

I'd always brushed off the idea of consistently needing to look your best as legitimate because sometimes, it seemed like it didn't matter. I thought *people should like me for who I am, not how I am dressing or what my facial hair looks like at any given moment.*

Let me tell you how wrong I was and how I learned I could make twice as much money simply based on the shirt I wear.

When I first started selling cell phones in a retail store, the company provided us with work shirts that had a logo on them. Every quarter, our shirt would be a new color, so we would all match, and with updated shirts, we all looked better, too. Management selected colors that matched the season of the year or changed the logo placement. In general, these shirts were decent quality but not the most comfortable.

In addition to our shirts changing regularly, we dealt with company policy changes. Any time a new executive leader came into our region, our process or system would change. Sometimes how we sold or what we were focusing on selling at the time would change. Sometimes we had to greet people at the door differently or stand in a different place in the store when we were not helping a guest. Every new high-level leader wanted to come in and make changes to try to initiate a new level of success, make a name for themselves, and justify why they got their job. Some of the changes helped, and some didn't, but the one that made the most significant impact of any I can remember from that period was when they initiated a shirt and tie requirement.

This was a fantastic transformation in the store. First, we started taking ourselves a little more seriously. We came in feeling and acting a little differently. We communicated more professionally and organized our desks/workstations. We took more care in how we shaved or did our hair. Ultimately, we leveled up. But the most significant difference was the immediate change in how the clients coming into the store treated us.

If you have ever been to a Verizon retail store, you know it can get a little crazy and hectic. It was even worse ten years ago when online account management was not a thing. People would come in for billing issues, technical service, phone issues, and typically they were not very happy. I would say to an angry person, "Sir, you dropped your phone in water, and that is why it is not working. And unfortunately, you do not have insurance, so I cannot replace it." That never went over well.

Once we switched to the shirt and tie combo, the way customers treated us and accepted feedback and suggestions was different. The way they communicated and appreciated us was different. Even clients who had been coming into the store for years interacted more positively with us. It blew me away that a simple change of appearance could make people act so different.

This change of perception helped me double my sales even though I used the same methods I always had. Nothing had changed about how I helped people. Nothing had changed about what I was selling to them. The *only* thing that changed was the way I dressed.

It is crazy the amount of power that your image has on people's perception of value.

That is why I am dedicating an entire chapter to this lesson.

The value we place on things is based on how we perceive them. That is why, as the saying goes, "One man's trash is another man's treasure." How we value things also relates to how we judge ourselves—and we do that just as much as we judge others. Anyone who has put on a sports or military uniform or merely a suit for work knows you feel better and are more confident and prepared.

It's the same as when you gain weight, don't have your hair cut, and your beard is growing wildly; you don't feel good about yourself. I don't care what you say to others about your appearance, when you slack, you silently judge yourself. Your judgment is also based on how you think others will perceive you. Sometimes these feelings are conscious, but many times, they are subconscious, and it is these thoughts that can derail your entire day.

Don't believe me?

Spend an entire week in sweatpants, a tee-shirt, and sandals. Then spend the next week in khakis, polo or a button-up, and decent shoes.

The difference in how you feel will be undeniable. And once you get control over how you look and how it makes you feel, you will have more control over how you perform—which will result in better compensation no matter your walk of life.

WHAT YOU WEAR

The biggest thing to remember about what you are wearing is that you can just as quickly overdress as you can underdress for a situation. And regardless of if you dress up or down, people will judge you based on how well you align with their values.

Let's say you recently graduated from law school at the top of your class. You got all the best grades and were involved in the most impressive extracurricular activities! Now, you are looking for a job at one of the top law firms in your city. You think you got it in the bag with your resume and accomplishments, so you show up to your interview in a tee-shirt, shorts, and flip-flops. Obviously, this does not align with the image of what an attorney at a top law firm in town would look like. And you can never get that first impression back. The entire interview could go awesomely, and the team could love you, but the inherent risk that you didn't dress correctly will linger on the minds of the decision-makers. You have become a potential liability because you showed poor decision-making and a lack of professionalism.

You can also overdress for an occasion. My ideal clients are construction companies and home remodelers now, but I also focused on appearance and matching my audience when I worked at Verizon. As a B2B sales rep, wearing professional business clothing was an expectation but not a mandate.

I'll never forget the meeting I had with one of my biggest clients. They were a plumbing company with around 200 employees, and I was working on closing a deal for all the new devices when I showed up to our first meeting in a suit. Luckily, I had no tie. My mindset was that I would stick with the expectations of my company and dress business professional regardless of what the client wore.

But I saw I had made an error in judgment as soon as I walked in. What my clients thought of my clothing choice was all over their faces. To them, I didn't understand who they were and was there to "sell" them something, not work with them to find the best solution. In their eyes, I was extremely overdressed, and in that moment, while they were assessing my wardrobe, I lost the little bit of a foothold I had earned with a few of the managers I'd spoken with before talking to the owner.

Understanding your audience is one of the most powerful accomplishments you can undertake in general, but this is especially true as it pertains to how you dress and speak. If you lose relatability with your audience for any reason, you are dead in the water because the person listening will never believe you truly understand them.

Early on, when I was launching my coaching business, I was complimented on the way I dressed. I was told that dressing in jeans and a polo or even shorts and a polo regularly was smart and helped me to be more relatable within the blue-collar industry. This person also said that a lot of coaches try to come in and act like they know more and are better than the business they are working with, and it just doesn't fly. Little did he know I'd already made that mistake and learned from it!

But how do you know how to dress?

Do your research! Call someone who knows the business or environment you are going into and ask them how you should dress or what the typical attire is. Check out a prospect's or business' online presence. See what their website says. Look at the headshots of the leadership team on their website or LinkedIn page.

If it is your first meeting or visit, don't be afraid to call ahead and ask someone there about what the typical attire is. Some people are afraid to make that call, but I assure you, more often than not when I made a call, the person on the receiving end was impressed that I would ask. It showed them that I cared.

Never has anyone treated me poorly because I asked about how I should look to match their environment.

Worst case scenario: dress in layers that you can take off to create a more casual look. Generally, all you need to do is take off your jacket and unbutton your cuffs to get you more in line with the audience. I always make a joke out of dressing down a little in an awkward moment to show I am personable and not afraid to pivot if necessary. A simple "Got that one wrong. Mind if I take this jacket off?" will help you align with the people in the room and break the ice. You are not perfect, so don't pretend you never make mistakes. If you can't admit when you are wrong—even when it comes to your dress—it makes you seem cocky instead of confident.

Realistically you will know someone at the meeting already, so start with the person you know when you take into account what to wear—but do not assume. Just like when you attend a wedding, you don't want to be the only one in a suit if everyone else is in beachwear.

One of the best lessons I have learned from mentors is to spend twice as much on half as much of your wardrobe.

Do this, and you'll always look better. Even if you wear the same thing regularly, you will look more polished. You will also save money because more expensive clothing lasts longer.

Ultimately it matters what you wear. There is a time and place for everything, and the better you get at understanding that, the better off you will be, and the easier it will be to make a great first impression. You can't close a deal in the first six seconds, but you can surely lose it.

BEING FIT MATTERS

I talked about exercise in the last chapter, but I want you to know that the reasons you exercise should extend to more than how it makes you feel. We all feel more confident when we look good. We all think more clearly and operate at a higher level when we get our blood moving regularly. But whether we partake in exercising or not affects the way others think of us. When we don't exercise, we might be viewed as a person who can't be taken seriously.

Being fit shows the world around you that you can dedicate yourself to maintaining a goal over a long period consistently. You broadcast that you pay attention to detail and are willing to work for it. It shows people you appreciate and respect yourself, and that makes others feel as if you will be more likely to recognize and appreciate them.

Anyone who has worked to get fit knows how hard it is to obtain and maintain it. Sticking to diets and making time to work out regularly is tough and requires a lot of sacrifices and mental toughness. This approach to your health and your resultant appearance influences how people respond to you—even when you simply walk into a room. People who are fit usually walk a little taller and smile more. When you exhibit these characteristics, you show people that you will do the work necessary to accomplish the goal—any goal. Salespeople especially like to work with those who they believe can solve their problems—it doesn't matter what you sell either. If you show up and look the part physically, you have a better chance of winning the deal.

You don't need to have 5% body fat or large muscles. Just don't be the person whose gut hangs over their belt and who breathes heavy and sweats every time they walk up a flight of stairs. I was that guy. It isn't pretty.

THE THREE S', AKA SH*T, SHAVE, AND SHOWER

Your morning routine is essential and is a big part of keeping your hygiene in check. If you are getting up 15 minutes before you have to leave, you cannot stay consistent when it comes to your personal needs. The three S' is a standard operating procedure many have talked about, and maybe you use it already. But if not, I encourage you to look at your routine first and see what you are missing before you implement the whole thing. Likely, you just need to get up earlier so you can accomplish the necessary good hygiene practices. Also note, if your breath stinks, your teeth are yellow, your hair is all over the place, and you need to shave, you will not be taken seriously. Looking unprepared will cause you to start behind the eight-ball and severely reduce your likelihood to dominate any situation.

As I have talked about, you have six seconds to make a first impression. The person you are interacting with will surmise an entire back story about you based solely on how you look. They will decide in their head if they should trust you or not. They will determine how much of a risk it would be to hire you, date you, or buy what you have to sell. Anything you do that gives them doubt will hurt your chances of winning.

I have seen people from all walks of life who do not take personal hygiene seriously. That said, I have never seen successful people who never brush their teeth and hair. Regardless of where you are in life, to get to the next level, you need to start taking care of your hygiene, what you wear, and how in shape you are. You want to avoid objections that people will have about you before deciding if they can trust you.

The one appearance pet peeve that has always bugged me the most concerns people in the restaurant industry. Men and women alike, no matter how high-end the restaurant, just don't do their hair. It isn't everyone who slacks on their hair, but often, you will see a waitress with her hair in some sort of messy bun thrown on top of her head. Or you will see waiters who look like they haven't shaved in days, their hair growing in spotty all over their neck.

I worked in the restaurant industry for a short time and know all about working late nights and days on end. It is exhausting. But you do need to have enough energy to take care of the little things. Most of the time I go out to a restaurant, I am going for the experience more than the food. A big part of that experience is interacting with the waitstaff. If they are not put together in the front of the house (the dining area), how well do you think the back of the house (the kitchen) is being taken care of by the staff?

The same goes for you in any situation where you are trying to win over an audience. Whether you're dealing with a job interview, client, or spouse, it doesn't matter! You have to show that you care about yourself before anyone can believe that you care about them.

If you cannot present a well-put-together front of the house (what you look like), people will judge the back of the house (how you think and make decisions) harshly.

If you don't understand the power of all of that, let me explain it a little differently.

Do you know why overcoming objections is so hard?

An objection happens when someone decides against what you are selling. The decision-maker is putting their foot down and saying no, using one of many reasons to articulate their refusal to work with you. Sometimes you won't even know the real reason because people are great at making up excuses that won't hurt your feelings. We have all done that at some point. We have all used the excuse "It's not you, it's me!" to avoid stating the real reason.

When someone makes a decision, they believe that decision is right, and when they have an objection to you, you now have to convince them they are wrong. Changing a person's mind is the most challenging communication task. That is why I do everything I can to avoid objections instead of needing to overcome them continually.

The reality is that if you do not look good, you won't feel good, and others won't feel good about you either. When you land yourself in this circumstance, you will have to change the minds of the audience. The challenge for many is that the audience you need to overcome is yourself. It's you looking in the mirror and subconsciously deciding what you are and are not capable of based on how you look.

That decision you make about yourself is so powerful that it affects your entire ability to perform, and when you can't perform at your highest potential, you cannot win as often. Luckily, you have full control over changing your self-image. Most of the time, when you embark on doing this, it just means that you need to be more disciplined in what you wear, how you work out, and how consistent you are in your hygiene. Decide today that a change is necessary, set a plan to make the change, and prepare for what is needed to make that change happen. Then for God's sake, follow through on it! Do it for you, and you will find that others will follow along and view you differently!

If you can do all of that effectively, you will see how much easier it is to become known, liked, and trusted. As we all know by now, becoming trusted is the accomplishment that will get people to provide you what you want.

In short, people can know and like you, but if they don't trust you, they won't buy whatever it is you are selling.

CHAPTER 7

GETTING KNOWN, LIKED, AND TRUSTED

Consistency is the true foundation of trust.
Either keep your promises or do not make them.
—Roy T. Bennett

It does not matter how great you are or how great your product or services are if no one knows you.

If your market or audience does not know you, they surely can't like you. And if they don't know and like you, it's impossible to get them to trust you.

But being liked is not always a necessity if you want to be trusted. Then again, if you can't be trusted, your ability to win will be hindered!

I was at lunch with some buddies, and we got to talking about whether it's better to be liked or trusted when it comes to business and sales.

The obvious answer is that a combination of both is ideal, but if you had to pick one, which would it be? Which would have a more significant impact on a client's buying decision? Between being trusted and liked, what do you use to determine who you put your faith, funds, or business success in? There is never a definite answer to questions like this because each buying environment, decision process, and impact is different, but here is what I took away from that lunch conversation.

First, it comes down to the product or service. If I'm buying a product like a TV or a set of dinner plates, the trust factor is less important. I don't need to trust someone if I want to buy the product because the inherent risk is lower. You're genuinely purchasing trust in the product—not the person selling it to you. If you're staring at the giant wall of TVs at Best Buy, how much you trust the guy manning that department is not a deciding factor in whether you will purchase anything or not. You'll probably make a decision based on the value of the brand, the features, size, and picture quality. If the Best Buy employee walks up and is super friendly and knowledgeable, you'll likely take advice from him, but your trust is in the brand, not the person.

Now let's say you're trying to find an investment banker. Whether or not I want to have a beer with the person is not as important as whether or not I trust him with my money. We all have friends who we love being around and hanging out with, but you would not want to do business with them. On the flip side, you don't want to deal with an asshole you are not friends with just because he is the best. Balance is necessary to make a business relationship work.

As a sales professional, the overall lesson you need to learn about being known, liked, and trusted is this: no matter what you're selling, don't just tell people what you think they want to hear or what you think will get them to buy because you will lose trust and credibility. Buyers are more informed now than ever before, and they know when you are full of shit. Even when they don't like the answer you give them when they ask you a tough question, they will appreciate you more when you give them complete and honest answers, which they can use to make informed decisions.

What I have found in 15-plus years in sales is that when I act like someone I would want to buy from, I win more. Focusing on being the type of person I would do business with has drawn in more people who relate to me and communicate the way I do. They are likely people who appreciate similar things and hold the same values. When I conduct business in this way, it also allows me to push people away who do not think, act, and communicate like me. We have all endured those types of people who make you feel like they are always analyzing, judging, and pushing back on everything you say. That happens because you portrayed a quality to them that they didn't think they could trust.

When I pretend to be someone other than myself, I'm not a match to what I think my audience is expecting. So, I fail more. It's that simple. The age-old saying applies here: "Treat others like you want to be treated." I'm sure that if you were making an important decision, you would want an objective view of the pros and cons. That is all your clients want, and sometimes, if not all the time, that means disclosing information that might cost you the sale. When you do this consistently, the more significant win is that you will gain a person's trust and become a valued asset. You can also become the go-to person when your sphere of influence needs to hear the truth, and doing this holds way better value long-term than telling someone what they want to hear when it isn't entirely true. Besides, when you are not honest, people will find out, and then you will lose all credibility.

Here's a sample of what might be said during a private conversation with a client. These conversations occur when you're not completely transparent. In each of these situations, trust has been lost. Do any of these questions or statements ring a bell for you?

"What do you mean it doesn't have that feature?"

"Why didn't Mike tell me about that when I asked him point-blank? If he didn't know for sure, he should have just told me and looked it up or something!"

"I mean, I like Mike, but I'm not sure I can trust him anymore. I guess I'll have to call Jeff next time. I don't love working with Jeff, but he always tells me the truth."

And here are some examples of things clients say during conversations that might occur when you are completely transparent.

"Man, it sucks that it doesn't have that feature. I swear it did, but I am glad Mike warned me!"

"That was nice of him to point me in the right direction to one of his competitors that can help me."

"I owe Mike a big one, and I will try to send him some business!!"

Do you see how if you are not transparent, one client can turn into zero clients just as quickly as being fully transparent can turn into several?

Transparency and vulnerability are very subjective, and a client's perception and dialogue in conversations around these topics could go 1,000 different ways. I'm sure you have either heard someone say those things or said them yourself at some point in your life. You may not hear these comments all the time, but you probably do hear them more often than necessary!

HOW TO GET KNOWN

Getting known is easier now than ever before. You have a great advantage today because you can be on dozens of platforms consistently to get known quickly. And when I say "being known," I mean having the ability to create awareness about you, your product, or your service.

There is no excuse for you not to be visible.

The more people see you, the greater the ability to make sales. Your visibility can come from a social media ad, a meetup or networking event, mailers or print ads, billboards, prospecting, emails, direct messages, and more.

There is no one specific place or media where you need to be seen, but you do need to be seen by the right audience to build awareness that will help you win. As you are putting yourself out there more, your audience also needs to understand you as they get to know you. People buy people, not products. If you believe people will buy your stuff by merely seeing a picture of it on your website or social media, look at Nike. Nike did $23.3 billion in shoe sales in 2020.[2] If people bought products alone, Nike wouldn't need Lebron James, Michael Jordan, or Tiger Woods. Nike would not need anything but a pair of shoes in every commercial. But Nike includes athletes and all sorts of people in their media.

People build relationships with people because of the way the person makes them feel. Nike knows people want to be like top athletes and celebrities, so they put their product on them and show it off. They are targeting a broad international audience while letting you know you can be the Lebron James or Tiger Woods of your city or town.

Many of us target a city or region and learn that it does not take much to build an audience of people who know you. But no matter the advantage you have nowadays or the target area, you have to get your face and voice out there so people can build an awareness about you.

---

[2] "Revenue from footwear segment of Nike, Adidas and Puma from 2010 to 2020 (in billion U.S. dollars", Statista, accessed July 1, 2021, https://www.statista.com/statistics/278834/revenue-nike-adidas-puma-footwear-segment/.

Now, before we go any further, let me guess the objection in your head: you don't like the way you look on camera!

Let me ask you this:

- Do you make in-person sales?
- Do you work with your clients at any point in person?
- Are you seen regularly in the community you serve?

Your public face and the face you put in front of your clients is the same face you put on camera. The only difference is that you can see it on camera, but the secret is that you are not your ideal client. You are not the person most likely to buy whatever it is you are selling. That means your opinion of your face is irrelevant to the overall process. The bottom line is if you are face to face with your target market at any point in the sales process, you need to be face to face with them through your online presence. SO, GET ON VIDEO TALKING ABOUT WHAT YOU DO KNOW!

I am not saying go out and create a bunch of new content. I am saying document what you already do every day. Talk about what you do every day already. Document it in a way that lets people see you operate better than your competition without coming out and saying to your audience, "I operate better." Share the way you think, the way you problem-solve, and the way you communicate. These are all your most significant unique factors that create your real competitive advantage.

Share the biggest lessons you've learned and the most significant problems you solve. At the end of every day for years, I would sit in my car in my driveway and ask myself these questions:

1. What is the biggest lesson I learned today?
2. What is the biggest problem I solved today?

These two questions helped me develop an entire content strategy, so I knew what I needed to talk about. If today's clients are dealing with a particular issue, it is very realistic to believe tomorrow's prospects will be as well!

If you are never face to face with your audience, imagine the competitive advantage you would have if you started building a relationship with your market as a person and not just a voice on the other side of the phone. You would crush your competition because people would start to build a relationship with you as a person, not just a brand.

The name on the back of your jersey is way more valuable than the logo on the front. And we know that the power of building a personal brand is proven all the time when great salespeople move companies. I can speak to the power of this because I had to go through it myself. When people build a relationship with you as a person, the brand you represent becomes a lot less critical. I have even seen this when companies go through a name or brand change. They don't lose any clients because their clients had built a relationship with the person, not the brand.

Now you might argue, "Mike, I'm the CEO. I don't want people to know *me*."

I get this, especially if you are planning to sell your business. If this is the case, then have someone on your team do the online awareness work or in-person networking. Your brand needs to be known by name. And not the brand name but the actual name of the person who works there. That person becomes the face of the brand who people will begin to like and want to give their business to.

So how do you get known enough to leave an impression?

You have to be different, unique, and entertaining. People go to social media for the entertainment factor. People look for the unusual stuff that is unlike the rest. When they see content like that, they stop scrolling. When they see similar messages coming from you in person, they will remember you. So just be yourself. You are your competitive advantage because no one does anything precisely as you do. Let that work for you instead of second-guessing everything you do. Don't stop being you because of how people might perceive you.

As I noted earlier, the best chance you have at winning and your greatest chance to be happy is to be exactly who you are. Don't hide from your truth because people will see right through what you are doing. If you have ever seen someone on camera reading a script, you know what I mean. It seems so rehearsed and fake. You know you are not seeing the real person. Once you figure it out, you move on because you want to build relationships with real people. I don't want that to happen to you, so be authentic.

You can do this with pictures, video, audio, and in your writing. Just make sure it is your face, your voice, and your words that people see. Creating a character that people can relate to is very powerful and creates fantastic long-term value.

I am sure you follow someone on social media right now, who if you saw them at the airport, you would walk right up to them and say, "hi" like you were friends—even though they've never met you. That is how powerful being yourself and consistently putting your brand out there can be. It doesn't matter how big or small your market or audience is. If you have one follower, you are an influencer, so just be yourself and watch your audience fill up with people who relate to you.

If you have been operating in your market for an extended period without putting your face out there, you need to take this plunge. Even if you have been around for decades and you think you don't need to, you are more wrong than the new guy. I have seen businesses doing around a million in revenue gain millions more dollars in revenue by getting online and showing their face. Becoming more known amongst their small town doubled their business in the first year.

The thing to keep in mind is that the majority of people who need you don't need you *right now*. They are not at the crossroads of making a buying decision immediately. That is why you have to be consistent with your advertising, or you might as well not do it. You need to be out there, so when a need does arise, you are top-of-mind. The average consumer's memory is about 30 minutes. When they see a video of yours, for instance, they might think it is awesome and love everything about you. But within half an hour, they will forget about you. Then in a few months, when they are ready to buy whatever it is you are selling, they will rack their brains to remember whoever they most recently saw. When trying to make a decision or retrieve a referral from our minds, we have all asked ourselves, *who was that guy we liked?* Or *what was the name of that restaurant we wanted to try?*

People do not forget you out of spite or with any intent to hurt you. The average consumer just forgets. It is your job to get and stay in front of people who may want your product or service down the road. Especially in today's environment where consumers want the freedom to do their research and take their time to make a decision, you must do this. You don't want people not to be aware of you because when they make the decision to move forward with a product or service, they want it immediately—and you want them to recall your words and your face. Thank you, Amazon, for creating such an unrealistic expectation for everyone's clients!

Let's say you are not internet-friendly, or you don't want to put your face on camera. Then you better get your networking game on point. In this case, you need to get in front of people just the same as you would get in front of your followers online. By now, most cities have so many meetups and networking groups that it can be overwhelming. I suggest being tactical with your time. When you increase your networking, it will be challenging to determine what is and is not a valuable group or person to spend your time going after.

In Charlotte, you can network four meals a day, seven days a week. I focus on groups intended to bring value. You might find that many groups are more social in nature. People might want to get together after hours and be more like drinking buddies than powerful connections. No offense, but I network for revenue, not friends. I do hope that business associates turn into friends, but I don't go out looking for friends and hoping they turn into business associates. I try to keep my time structured, and I am not looking for more opportunities away from my family that will not bring me value worth my investment.

Do your research. I suggest visiting a few different groups at different times of the day and in different locations. You will need to find one that will work for you consistently and that has a group of people you believe can bring value to your mission. It doesn't matter whether your mission is to sell construction projects or any other product or service. You need to find an outlet you can regularly attend where you can give as much value as you receive.

I also caution against joining too many groups. When you do that, it is tough to bring a significant enough benefit to any of them. You only have access to so many opportunities to refer business to others, so if you spread it amongst several groups, it'll be hard to bring enough worth to any one person and get great value in return.

The bottom line is if you don't start building relationships in person and online, you are going to get passed over or beaten by someone who does. It doesn't matter how good your work is. If you are not creating an audience, you are going to lose out to someone else who has done the work to create theirs.

So, get over yourself and realize what makes you unique makes you more relatable and draws in the right people to your audience. Market yourself consistently, and you will become known as well as earn the right to become liked and trusted.

HOW TO GET LIKED

There is no specific tactical guide to being liked. There is no recipe that states if you are in enough of the right places, people will become aware of you and will like you. Getting liked is a lot more subjective.

Let me tell you this hard truth. Fifty percent of people won't like you if you are true to yourself, and that is great. Because if you can be yourself, the other 50% will love you. However, if you are on the fence, trying to be what everyone likes, no one will like you!

If you can't be true to who you are, many people, if not everyone, will see right through you. They will not like the fact that depending on what room you are in or who you are around, you are a different person.

Despite everything I just talked about, there is still a time and place for everything—and you need to know the rules of the game. You can't cuss in church, and it doesn't make sense to sit quietly at a football game. You have to understand your audience to know how to deliver who you are and what you believe in. The way you give your message to your audience cannot change from moment to moment.

Stick to your morals and values at all times, even if it causes some people not to like you. It's okay if that happens, and you should actually expect that. When you are comfortable with who you are in every situation of your life, it will make others love you. That is a hell of a lot better than having everyone unsure of who you are and what you stand for—which leads to them not liking you at all.

First, work to maintain your belief system, then get to work getting people to like you by giving. You will see that the more you invest in other people and their causes or priorities, the quicker they will like you.

After years of being in the corporate world, I learned the best way to gain respect through your first impression is to start every conversation with eye contact and a handshake. Now with the complexities of the pandemic of 2020-21, I try to make my content, videos, and Zoom calls as inviting and personal as possible. One big change I made was trying to be more intentional with eye contact with the camera, so the audience feels like you are looking right at them whether they are watching on their phone or on a big screen at an event. Proper and professional introductions are becoming less and less common. Generally, and once we get back to in-person events, people appreciate eye contact and a solid handshake. So, put your phone away and pay attention to the person in front of you. Nothing bugs people more than feeling like they do not have your attention, especially if you are looking at your phone. Set it down or leave it in the car. Then you can focus on the person in front of you.

Paying attention seems simple, but so many people working events and chatting with people they don't know online ask just enough questions to try and sell you on whatever they are selling. I've observed this a lot: a person will talk to another person at an event, but the person who is supposed to be listening is obviously teeing up the next questions in their head—before the other person is even done talking.

A person loses interest in a conversation if they believe you are not going to be a buyer. When you approach every person you meet with an agenda first before you try to get to know and help them, it causes them not to like you.

Instead, ask questions and sincerely listen. Care enough to ask and hear what they have to say instead of thinking of what to ask or say next.

The easiest way to do this when getting to know people is to start every conversation with, "What do you do, and how can I help you?" When they answer, spend time listening and then actually do what they said would help them. I see so many people drop the ball in this situation, but if you handle yourself right, this can be one of the easiest and most effective ways for people to like you. Please focus on actually delivering on the help they are asking you to give. This could come in the form of an introduction, feedback, or just offering to get them to one of your events.

I have told someone exactly what I wanted them to do to help me hundreds of times after they asked, but then they didn't follow through. After going through this a few too many times, I have realized people generally don't expect you to deliver on what you said you were going to do for them. That was also when I realized that follow-through created a significant gap in networking. Knowing this, I focused on being the guy who delivered.

Doing that will separate you from others because people will realize you are there to help others before helping yourself. That is a fast way to become liked. It is much different than the typical engagement experience that usually happens with someone new.

While we're on the topic of assisting others, make sure you give your time to organizations and causes. If you are a part of a formal group, get involved with their board or leadership. Most charities are always on the lookout for people to take on responsibility. Offering to help them is a great way to show that you are likable. Just make sure that you take your offer to help seriously. If you volunteer and never show up or never do what the job requirements call for, you will hurt yourself and your reputation. Their admiration at putting yourself out there will turn into, "He is a great guy, but in my experience, he doesn't typically follow through." Not only will your reputation take a hit, you will also likely let a lot of people down. They will become frustrated with you, and that will hurt your chances of being liked, too.

The more you volunteer and deliver on what you are being asked to do, the more you are liable to follow through. So, take your pledge to help seriously, and you will see a return on your investment in improved respect and reputation.

Giving of your time is one of the best things you can do to be liked within your community. Most people know that time is precious, and when you are willing to donate your time to an event or cause, it is appreciated.

We will dig more into the Rule of Reciprocity later in the book but know that this rule is one of the quickest ways to be liked and appreciated.

When you are a business owner who gets all your value from your community, you have to give back. It is rarely money that creates the most significant impact on your market. People need to take on responsibilities that create change. They need to put on events or simply be present as a body available to lend a hand at festivals. It is ten times more valuable for you as the business owner to be at an event helping than if you just had a banner there.

Again, people build relationships with people, not banners. The minute someone decides you look likable, they hold onto that impression until you prove otherwise. When people see you hand out drink tickets at brewery events or operating the gate at a summer festival, they will feel like you are a part of the community just like them—and that influences them to like you.

The more you invest, the greater your return. Becoming liked is the best endeavor to spend your time and attention on. Give people your attention and genuinely let them know that you want to help them when you meet them. Follow through on what you say and then go out into your community and volunteer your time and expertise. The more you give of yourself, the faster you will be liked.

HOW TO BECOME TRUSTED

Getting to a place of trust is the pinnacle of any relationship that changes the game completely. Once someone decides they can trust you, their comfort in referring others to you or engaging with you at all ascends to a whole new level.

But how do you get there?

Building trust starts by doing everything I talked about in the previous sections. To reiterate, being liked is not always a prerequisite to being trusted, although you must do a few things well to earn the right to be trusted.

You have to be willing to sacrifice what you think is best for you for what is best for the situation. We are often put into situations where we have to decide between what is best for us right now compared to what is best for the overall mission. Your ability to put your ego off to the side without having to be right not only shows that you can be trusted with tough decisions. It shows that you believe those around you. It is important to be open to feedback from the people you spend the most time with because it will keep them wanting to help you. In a sense, you get what you give a lot of the time. If you are constantly second-guessing and overriding those around you, they will treat you the same way.

Imagine you are in a situation where a project for a client got messed up, but it was unclear exactly whose fault it was. You could play the "he said, she said" game and try to get the client to fix it. Or you could take ownership and bite the bullet because anything that happens on the job site or within a project is your responsibility and needs to be repaired at your expense. You can't always eat the cost, but being able to take ownership of any situation and dealing with the consequences of it will help you build trust with the people around you.

If people know that you are going to own it no matter the outcome, they are more likely to trust you. To be honest, most people don't want to take ownership of situations. Putting yourself at the front of the pack, taking control, and owning the task to completion lets people around you know you can be trusted. Look for opportunities to take control and don't be a 99%-done kind of person. Be an I-know-you-will-get-it-done kind of person.

Regardless of how you endeavor to gain trust, you have to be willing to solve problems, whether they are your problems or not. If a duty needs doing, you have to be ready to step in and get it done. Sometimes this is not fun, and it costs you time and money, but at the end of the day, do you want to be the person who people can rely on? Or do you want to be the person who everyone likes even though they know you never take responsibility for anything?

I think you know the answer.

The biggest and most important impact you can make occurs when you are consistent. I have talked a lot about consistency in this chapter because it is the most critical undertaking that will encourage people to trust you. People don't like taking risks, and if they don't know which version of you they are getting on any given day, they simply won't trust you.

It is essential to be consistent in how you speak, what you say, what you look like, and how you respond. We have all met the person who leaves you unsure as to which version of them you are going to get that day.

I was that person for a period of my life, and I still struggle with letting that go to an extent. I wear my emotions on my sleeve, so sometimes I am emotional, short, and angry. I have worked on it, but as a very passionate person, I tend to let the passion take over sometimes. When I was not good at controlling my feelings for my audience, I am sure people were unsure of which Mike they were going to get that day. I am not perfect and never claim to be, but I do try.

Being in control of my outward appearance is something I will continue to focus on because I do not want my impact in life to be minimized by other people's first impressions of me. When I look the part, I instill trust in others; when I don't, it leaves room for second-guessing, and I do not have time for people to second guess me on this journey.

You also have to be consistent in how you represent yourself online. Your brand, whether it is a business or your personal brand, needs to be consistent across all platforms. Your website can't tell a different story than your social media, and your social media can't express a different quality than you personally deliver when you speak.

You have to make sure your online presence represents the quality of the person you are and the experience you deliver!

In today's environment, no matter the media we are talking about, you need an online presence. It's the only way that people will take your brand seriously because it is where people go to confirm what they heard about you from former and present clients and even through your network!

BE THE SAME IN PERSON AND ONLINE

Let me run a scenario by you to show the power of being consistent both in-person and online. I am going to use a remodeler as my example because that is the audience I work with every day. But as you are reading this example, please put your clients into the story.

Let's say you just completed a fantastic kitchen remodel project for your client Paul. From start to finish, Paul was incredibly happy with you, your team, and the quality of your work. Because of that, Paul refers you to his neighbor Steve.

In a best-case scenario, you have an online presence that matches the experience Paul had. So, when Steve looks you up online to research you and sees this strong presence, he will believe Paul's recommendation and likely hire you. That's because you represent a lower risk as compared to hiring someone he doesn't know who he wouldn't be able to ask around about to gauge whether he should trust their experience.

So, you work on Steve's project and knock it out for him as well. Now you have two referral partners, testimonials, and champions of your brand—all because you built consistent systems and processes.

More often than not, that is *not* what I see happen with contractors working in (insert whatever field you work in here).

Usually, what happens is Paul refers you to Steve. Then Steve looks you up online, but your website is outdated, and you have not posted on Facebook or Instagram in months. The lack of regular content plants a little concern in Steve's mind, but he still calls you and sets up a meeting to look at his kitchen project.

On the day of the meeting, you get busy on a job site dealing with a sub, so you show up late to your in-home consultation. When you get there, you are carrying the frustration from that sub-issue and are not on your best game. You are a little short and not very attentive.

The sales meeting with Steve goes okay, but he feels like meeting you does not line up with what Paul has said about you. The gap in the expectation between what Paul said you were like and what Steve experienced plants another seed of concern in his mind that creates objections.

Next, you take longer than expected to get the proposal to Steve. So, Steve has to follow up with you to find out when he will get it. Now, Steve is starting to question everything about your process and attention to detail.

Because Paul referred you, Steve still hires you. But the project hits some bumps in the road, runs late, and is over budget. Now Steve is pissed. He is upset with you, but he is more upset with Paul for referring you.

Steve is so frustrated that he takes it up with Paul and asks, "Is this the experience you had?"

Paul is upset now because he looks terrible to his neighbor, and this will make Steve start to question Paul's ability to make decisions and refer him to quality people.

When all is said and done, instead of having two champions of your business, you now have two people who are incredibly frustrated with you because you could not deliver a consistent client experience. Paul and Steve have both lost their ability to trust you enough to refer you to other neighbors. Worse, they take their complaints online and post in their neighborhood group that you do good work, but you are challenging to work with and are inconsistent.

You can see, as illustrated through these scenarios, that it doesn't matter what industry you are in or what product or service you are offering. I am sure you have witnessed similar experiences and challenges and maybe even experienced them yourself. That had nothing to do with your ability to do a great job, but everything to do with your ability to do an excellent job *consistently* in such a way that your market is led to trust you. That is why you see some businesses flourish and others die out. Typically, this has nothing to do with their quality and more to do with how consistently they deliver an exceptional client experience.

First, be known. Then focus all your efforts on investing time and money into being liked and trusted. When you do this, you will see massive returns over time as your market grows a relationship with you.

In multiple industries full of competition and people promising the world, it is rare to find someone who can be known, liked, and trusted.

Be that person for your market, and you will win in the long run.

Once you have these three steps cemented into place, it's time to build on them. In the next chapter, I will tell you a story of the power of follow-through and why it needs to be part of every decision you make!

CHAPTER 8

THE IMPACT OF FOLLOWING THROUGH

It only takes one "Ah, shit" to kill ten "Atta boys."
—*Dom Claudio*

It could take you weeks, months, or even years to build trust with your market. It will involve dozens or even hundreds of events that you attend to connect, engage, and deliver to the people around you. It doesn't matter if you are an entrepreneur or intrapreneur; you have to sustain consistency over time to become known, liked, and trusted, as outlined in the last chapter.

So, why is it so difficult for people to follow through on what they say they are going to do? That simple mistake, as innocent as it is, will destroy all the work you have put into a relationship. Trust me; I have done it.

IN SALES

Having all the right motives and a big heart isn't all that's necessary to win. Yes, these qualities are a big part of winning, but let me share with you how they can also get you into trouble!

Once I had a great referral partner who sent me multiple six figures' worth of work over a year's time. It took me about two years to gain this person's trust, and once I did, they sent me some of the best projects we'd had that year. We had a great relationship going until I messed it up all because of good intentions but shitty follow-through.

This person had connected me with one of their best connections—a person who was very important to them—and asked me to help them out. From the first conversation, I knew that the project was probably going to be too small for us, but because my best referral partner asked me to do it, I said yes to an in-person meeting. I showed up and ran the meeting like I usually would, thinking the entire time, *this won't be worth my time*. I only took the meeting because I felt like I had to do it—which is never a great way to conduct business. As expected, the project was way below our average project size, so I took the information and told the client I would get back to them by the end of the next week. I had every intention of doing that, but as a salesperson and someone trying to grow a business, I got distracted with "higher priority" responsibilities.

Well, the end of next week rolled around, and I realized I had not even begun to work on it yet, so I emailed the new potential client to let them know I would need a little more time. I noted that some things had come up. Needing more time on a proposal or having something come up that pushes some to-do items out is not uncommon. Still, I think because of the mindset I had about the entire situation, the client felt like I was not taking them seriously or, at a minimum, not appreciating their time.

The client shot back an email that talked about how disappointed he was that I could not even pick up the phone and call them about the estimated delay and how I must not think their project is very important. I don't remember the entire email, but that was the gist of it. I brushed it off and tried to call to apologize, but again I was not taking that project seriously because it was more of a favor. I never heard back from that client. I pissed them off because I didn't deliver on what I said I would.

A few months later, I realized I had not heard from my referral partner, either. As a regular part of my process, I touch base with my referral partners every few months just to keep them up to date on what's going on with the business. When I called, I got an earful: "How could you let me down like that?" They asked me how I could take something or someone that was important to them and not handle it with the level of expectation I was capable of. Then my former referral partner told me that they had lost trust in their ability to refer any new connections to me, so they were no longer willing to do so. Losing this referral partner was my first major lesson in being honest, even if it meant losing the job and saying no to opportunities that just didn't fit me. I knew the power in saying no, but this was the first major lesson I had learned in how not following through on what I said I was going to do hurt more people than just me.

If I had explained that this referral was not a project for me and why it would benefit the client to talk to someone else, I could have referred them to another company that would have been happy to help them and would have done a great job.

Then I should have called the referral partner back and informed them of the decision I'd made and why. Keeping them informed would have given them what was needed so that they would still have trust in me. Ultimately, if I had just been honest about it, I would have kept that person informed and happy and been able to continue to benefit from the relationship and the referrals they brought into the company.

I learned what I should have done by handling other situations differently and being honest. Man, this approach worked better than anything else. People were impressed and sometimes blown away that I wasn't just chasing money but wanted to deliver the right experience every time. They appreciated that I was willing to say no when the opportunity was not right. As it pertained to me, I was ready to educate people on our process and take the time to guide them to a solution that was best for them, even if it was not me.

Understanding that when people call, they are looking for an answer to their problems but that the solution doesn't need to be you may sound like an obvious lesson to many. But as an entrepreneur, you have to learn it at some point.

That simple misstep of trying to do more than I should have and then not following through cost me hundreds of thousands of dollars directly—and who knows how much indirectly. I lost years of effort in building my know, like, and trust factor and blew it all away with one mistake, one decision, and one phone call. All the effort I had invested was ruined.

It's not only in sales that you can lose by not following through or setting expectations you cannot deliver on.

WITH FRIENDS

I mentioned that you could be liked but not trusted, and that happens when you are fun but unreliable. We all have those friends who we invite out, but we never know when they will show up. Or what about the friend who you asked to help you do something, but they didn't deliver on it? You won't cut them out of your life immediately, but over time, you'll start to filter what you trust them with.

The part most people miss and why so many, including me, end up losing relationships is that we don't realize how the little things add up. The small decisions you make that let people around you down but that are not big enough individually to make them say anything to you about it are significant. The little transgressions that by themselves are not impactful, but when you start to add them up, equal five or ten incidences over the years, destroy people's trust in you.

Being late to that one thing that you said you were going to—no big deal.

Forgetting to bring a dessert, you said you would—no big deal.

Getting a phone call or text message and not returning it for days or not at all—no big deal.

None of those things seem like a big deal, but when you add them up, you are planting seeds of unreliability. Your friends will start to second guess you when you ask them for favors or need help. You will become that person people are happy to have around, but who not much is expected from. Now, many people like that level of responsibility, but if you want to win in life, you have to be reliable. You have to be the person people think of when they need something done. Or the person who is the go-to when a job needs to be done right. Being a stand-up person is a more significant responsibility, and it requires reliability to sustain it.

Another big reason you want to make sure you follow through with what you say concerns how you make the other person feel about themselves when you drop the ball. Many of us deal with self-worth issues. I am someone who has dealt with mental illness for the majority of my life. Whether fair or not, people who deal with self-worth issues place incredible value on how others commit to them.

When someone lets me down, I don't blame them; I blame myself.

I assume the reason they didn't get back to me is not that whatever they did instead was very important. I believe that *I* was not important enough.

I promise you there are people in your life who feel the same. When you don't follow through, they blame themselves. They assume you don't care about them or that they are not important enough for you to commit to consistently.

Often, someone following through and doing what they said they would, gives people value as well. When you are down, depressed, or anxious, someone saying through their actions that you are worth the effort to show up for is a lot louder than your words. You following through and being attentive to that other person could be the one thing needed to pull them out of the darkness.

If you flip the situation, that one person, even a stranger, showing up for you through their actions could be what turns the tides for you. It's just like how it hurts when someone says they will be there for you, but then they never actually are there for you—you feel it.

Actions speak worlds more than words. They will make or break a trust factor immediately. That is why so many unlikely relationships flourish. One person feels safe since the other person follows through for them. If this is you, and you are on the receiving end, that person has helped you validate your worth by being willing to be consistently there for you. I am not saying every person in your life is dealing with some sort of mental battle and needs you to be there every minute of every day. I am saying that you never know the impact following through on your commitments can have on someone's outlook and self-belief.

Go out of your way for someone this week and watch their reaction. I am sure it will light them up, and you will see a smile that lols and emojis can't describe.

IN BUSINESS

The days of "Do as I say, not as I do!" are long gone. If you have not adjusted, you are failing as a leader.

As a leader, you are an example for everyone who works for you. How you do things and how you communicate drives the culture of your entire team. This level of responsibility seems straightforward, but if you don't live up to the standards you have set forth for your organization, your team will never buy into what you say. We are all guilty of this.

As leaders, we are good at making excuses for ourselves on why things didn't get done, why we had to get to the job site, or why we had to deal with the bank or fight with a sub. We are good at expounding upon why the fire we had to deal with was more important than the commitment we made to our team.

- When you don't do what you say you will, a disconnect like the examples below occurs.

- You tell your employees that being on time is essential, but you always show up late to meetings.

- You tell your employees to make sure they are at the team meeting next week, but then at the last minute, you say you can't make it because of another priority.

- You give your employees a hard time for not responding to a call, text, or email, but you don't follow the same guidelines.

The minute you show your employees you are not prioritizing a project or task or giving it any attention, they won't either.

The actions you take to show your character influence the culture you want to create. Creating culture can be as simple as emptying a trash can or as significant as following one of your core values. Just as your kids follow your lead, so do your employees. It doesn't matter how big or small your business or team is. You are the true north for your organization.

I have heard so many leaders say something off-the-cuff about an employee appreciation day or about a possible raise or bonus and not deliver on it. And then I have seen employees get incredibly discouraged and broken down. Keep doing this over time, and your employees will be numb to anything you say or do because they won't believe a word you say anymore.

Even if you find yourself accidentally doing this and have the best intention to help motivate your team, you will still affect the people in your business negatively. Let's say that an event happened that got in the way and derailed your intentions. You may have lost a big client, incurred a sizable expense, or even gotten busy with a thousand tasks and forgotten you'd said anything. But I promise you that the audience to whom you pledged your promise did not forget. Drop the ball, and you will notice your team sitting around talking amongst themselves about that "imaginary bonus" the boss always talks about giving them. They might make a joke about how they will get that project done as soon as "employee appreciation day" happens. When you are a leader who shoots off your mouth with no follow-through, all your employees will have a good belly laugh about it because they know that day is never coming. In their minds, not hitting their deadline is justified.

As a leader who has no self-awareness of your lack of follow-through, you won't know mutiny in your culture is happening until it is too late. If you don't wake up and make some needed changes, one day, your entire culture will be destroyed. You definitely need to do the waking up yourself since, as the boss, no one will want to call you out on your bullshit. And in your team's eyes, you can do whatever you want anyway. Employees won't want to risk their jobs or upset management over something they don't have control over. Your team will crumble as more and more deadlines are missed and mistakes crop up frequently.

The next step is that you will confront the group about how you need them to be consistent and get more focused on the task at hand. Then right before your eyes, you will see all your team members thinking to themselves, *yeah, well, you never follow through on what you say you are going to do for us, so why should we commit so hard for you?* You will be confused as to why effort and performance are not improving until you realize it all stems back to you letting down everyone by not following through on what you said you were going to do. I don't care if it's as simple as filling the break room fridge with water or giving everyone a big bonus at the end of the year. Do NOT say it if you are not 100% confident that you can follow through on it.

Understandably, if you hold yourself accountable for following through consistently, you will have the opposite effect on your team. The people who work for you will work harder, longer, and more efficiently because you always deliver for them. This is akin to the Rule of Reciprocity and them feeling like they need to provide for you. Because you have still held up your end of the agreement, your team will not want to let you down. They will feel like they owe it to you.

But what do you do in a situation where you can't follow through or where you realize you dropped the ball?

When mistakes are happening and balls are dropping, I recommend full transparency, vulnerability, and ownership.

People can smell bullshit and a made-up excuse a mile away. When you walk in ready to tell a whopper, they can see on your face that you have rehearsed what you are going to say. And here's a tip: fabricated details don't make you appear less at fault. It doesn't matter if you need to come clean to a customer, friend, or employee. Being straightforward and vulnerable is the best tactic.

Tell the person you have wronged exactly what happened and how it happened. If you are embarrassed by the reason you dropped the ball, be honest, and then do some retrospective thinking about if you should have been doing what you are embarrassed by or not. Maybe you need to reevaluate your priorities in life. Perhaps you need to get refocused on the mission to ensure you are doing what is necessary to drive the right message.

Or maybe you just need to get better at using a calendar and keeping up with the responsibilities that need to get done. When it comes to my calendar, if an appointment is not on my schedule, it is not real to me. If a meeting or call is not blocked off on my calendar or task list, it has a small chance of getting done. If you are seeing a pattern of letting people down, I would suggest auditing how you manage your to-do list and that you find a solution ASAP.

The bottom line: do not commit to doing something unless you are sure you can get it done. Following through is one of the most powerful things you can do because it is becoming rarer to see people do it. If you miss something, be transparent and vulnerable about what happened and own up to it. When you take responsibility, you have a much better chance of receiving forgiveness. This is not guaranteed, but you will at least keep a reputation of honesty.

Now that you know how to become known, liked, and trusted as well as the importance of following through on what you say you are going to do, let me tell you about the final piece of building strong relationships.

If you want to win in life, you need a team of people around you. It has been said that being great at sales will help you make money, but your ability to communicate with, manage, and lead people can make you a fortune.

Stay tuned because, in the next chapter, I will dig into the knowledge that is needed to build strong relationships.

CHAPTER 9

BUILDING STRONG RELATIONSHIPS

You can make more friends in two months by becoming interested in other people than you can in two years by trying to get other people interested in you.
—Dale Carnegie

Isn't it amazing how a small shift in your perspective can make the most significant impact on your life?

Far too often in business and life, people get hung up on trying to make someone like them instead of focusing on how they can provide value in that person's life.

I have seen this frequently occur over the years.

PEOPLE ARE LIKE A BOX OF CHOCOLATES

Have you ever noticed someone suddenly change and become a completely different person depending on the environment they are in or the people they are around? We are all guilty of this to an extent, but some people go so far as to completely change what they believe in. They do this so the people around them will like them instead of focusing on how they can help others around them.

> **When you sit back and think of all the conversations you have throughout the day, how many times have you walked away knowing that you left the other person on the other end better off than when you met them?**

Dealing with people is a constant battle of two extremes that can take place in any situation. These two elements are also known as a dichotomy. A dichotomy is a contrast between two factors that are entirely different or are opposites. These two extremes are what you have to be careful of because you can get sucked into believing you are wrong or need to change. I have found over the years of dealing with the public in retail sales and working with homeowners on a regular basis that two people will respond completely differently to the same approach or process. You can use the same follow-up process with two people, and one will be thankful you were persistent, and another will cuss you out for being a nuisance. That doesn't mean your approach is wrong. It just is the basic dichotomy of dealing with the human element. If you do not have a belief in why you are doing what you are doing, it's easy to get discouraged and make changes when in fact, the only issue with the process was the differing responses you heard. You have to understand that is just a part of dealing with people. It's why you need to have a strongly defined process and why behind how you communicate.

When I am helping business owners make adjustments, I always say focus on the middle 80% of situations or clients. The top and bottom 10% should not be what you are basing your decisions on, especially in today's world of online opinions and keyboard heroes. Any time I am looking at documenting or changing a process, I base the expectations and standard operating procedures on how the "average" person would respond. Don't totally ignore the outliers, the top and bottom 10% of people you deal with but focus on the middle 80% of average interactions. There are always scenarios that don't fit the mold, but you don't want to use those when creating your standards.

One day you are too nice, and the next day you are too mean. Then you are too passive as well as too aggressive.

Add to that a constant variety of people and how they respond to you, and you can understand why dealing with the public is so difficult.

I learned pretty early on in my in-home sales career that you can say the same thing in the same way to ten people, and you will get seven different reactions. Some people will love you for how you are saying whatever your point is, and some will hate you for it. Still, others will have a stone face—they will give you zero reaction.

Working in retail or with the public is like opening a box of chocolates: "You just never know what you are going to get." It'll make you feel like Forest Gump and want to RUN!

This is a world where you have to judge a book by its cover to prepare yourself for how you should interact with the person in front of you.

And doing so has nothing to do with judging someone negatively. I want to urge you to rethink any judgment you might want to put on people. It benefits you to do a little recon on someone before starting a conversation with them so you can approach them in a way that minimizes the risk that you will upset them or say something that goes outside what they are expecting from you.

I talked about first impressions earlier in the book, but this is another reason to focus on your first impression. When building relationships, it is important that you portray an image that aligns with the way you want people to communicate with you. You know you have to interact with people differently because you will be making your first impression. So, you must also know that other people will react in different ways to you as well. People will make decisions about your personality, your value to the situation, and your ability to deliver on their expectations based on their first impression of you. So, when you meet people who you want to build a strong relationship with, it is important to review yourself and how you will come across in an initial meeting so you can avoid losing credibility and trust right off the bat. You can recover from this during an interaction, but I focus on trying to avoid as many objections as possible, especially when meeting someone for the first time.

Overall, dealing with people is a challenge. I say this a lot with my coaching clients because too many people adjust their approach or delivery on a regular basis because they put so much weight on how their previous clients reacted to them. They think, *well, it didn't work this time. I must need to try something different next time.* When you do this, you never know what is and is not working. It's like swinging a bat differently every time. You may make contact occasionally, but you'll never figure out what does and does not work for you. And you'll never get better at the way that works the best. You have to focus on fine-tuning your process over time. You are not trying to recreate it for each interaction, and you can't anyway because you lack the knowledge of what does and doesn't work.

If one person hates how you follow up on a proposal and you change your approach, then the person who loved the old way you were doing things won't be happy. If one person is annoyed by your small talk while another person is grateful for it and appreciates you taking the time to make them feel comfortable, if you change it, someone won't be happy.

Welcome to the trickiest puzzle in existence. When you deal with people for a living, you are continually trying to figure out who you are dealing with and what they are going to want from you. When is the right time to change or adjust your approach based on new information? When should you invest in someone, and when should you ask something of them?

When you learn to read people this way, you can focus more on what is important to them, which immediately makes you more relatable and likable. Building relationships is all about how you can become liked and trusted. I talk about this a lot throughout this book because, in your life, you are going to hit many obstacles, and having a large group of people who like and trust you gives you more people you can reach out to for help to overcome and win in that scenario.

Figuring out what to do is not as simple as it seems. If you stay true to yourself at all times, people will say you are rigid and difficult to please. But if you adjust and change your mind all the time, people will not know what you stand for. They will lose trust in you because they will not know what version of you they will get. Being able to change your mind is a compelling skill because it allows you to adapt to new information. It also allows you to make decisions quickly with limited data because you know you are capable of changing your mind later.

You can see how using your measuring stick to assess the responses of others can get you in trouble. If you put too much emphasis on others' opinions, you will never know when you are doing the right thing. If you put too little emphasis on them, you will never really connect with anyone. So, what are you supposed to do?

Before I can answer that question, I need to tell you that deciding what to do begins with realizing that you are not for every person. Everyone is not supposed to like you. Trying to be liked by everyone drives many people into a hole of misery.

I've definitely put more effort into the one person who doesn't like me than into the nine who do.

I fight with this because of the time I have invested in my business and in relationships. Because of what I have sacrificed to get to this place in my life, and because of all the times I have gone out of my way.

RELATIONSHIP ACCOUNTS

Ed Mylett once said something that made so much sense. After years of playing the fine line of, "What is too much and what is not enough?" Ed said, "What does the account look like?"

What he means is, "What is the equity in the relationship bank account of the person?" He made this analogy because, like a bank account, you cannot withdraw from it unless you have deposited into it and have maintained a balance.

Put another way: you can't ask for something and expect to not owe anything if you have not already given something.

It begs the question: are you giving more than you take?

Over the last few years, I've learned that the more you give, the more the universe returns to you. But what you get back will not always equate to a one-for-one response.

As you know by now, I always preach about following the process and how the results will follow.

In all aspects of my life, whether it was the gym, sports, sales, or leadership, it didn't matter. All I had to do to succeed was figure out the process and stick to it. When it comes to building relationships, I have built and stuck to a process, but it does not always pan out the same.

I can also break it down this way: when you make a certain number of sales calls, it typically equates to a certain number of sales. This is a pretty straight-forward equation. Knowing how many people you need to talk to in order to close a deal is the best way to reverse engineer how much work you need to do to hit your sales or revenue targets.

Building strong relationships is not as easy to track as the metrics in other aspects of your life. You can't track relationship building like you would your workouts or sales activity. So, I have always just said, "I am going to be a giver of my time, assets, skillsets, or knowledge." And I have always leaned on this idea: "If I continue to give, I will win." But I also know that if I do not provide to the person, I will not get back from them. Honestly, you can't look at rela-tionships that way, or you will end up let down more often than not. And you cannot give with the intent to receive. You just have to give.

Let me put this theory into a real-life scenario for you. When I first started leading people, I struggled to get buy-in. I would get frustrated because I would ask and ask and ask for things to be done, and I was pretty unsuccessful at making that happen in my first management job. I had moved into a role where I was coaching some of my previous peers who were doing a job that I was doing, so I knew what they were dealing with and the world they were living in. That being the case, I didn't have much empathy or patience for them. As a result, I just gave orders and expected them to happen.

Understand that when you give orders, you are pulling from the relationship account. What I didn't realize was that I had not deposited anything for these people. Just like any account, if you keep pulling money out without putting money in, eventually, your account gets shut off. That is the situation I had on my hands—a bunch of employees who were over my shit. They checked out, and I lost their buy-in because all I did was ask for them to do things and give orders.

What I learned later down the road was how to build people up and deposit into them. When you do this, you earn the right to ask something of others and to give them direct and honest feedback. Some of my best friends are the hardest on me, just like I am on them. One of the best things you can do for someone is expect more of them than they expect of themselves. It makes them better in the long run, even if they don't live the honest feedback in the moment. The point is that you have to earn the right to do that before you just start throwing around feedback to people.

Think about any person in your life right now.

There are certain people whose opinions you respect because they have invested in you in some way, shape, or form. They have complimented you, given you positive and valuable feedback, and have gone out of their way to help you with something. Because of this, they have earned the right to give you an honest critique or ask you to do something. You are a lot more likely to listen to them as opposed to the person who never has anything good to say, who has never gone out of their way for you, and who has never done something to create any kind of value for you. When that person comes knocking with advice, help, or critical feedback, you will likely blow them off.

I am sure each of us can say that we all had a leader who took the time to get to know us. That leader was there for you and genuinely cared for you and your family. That person probably asked questions about how you were doing or how you enjoyed your job. They may have gone out of their way to give you a project or a client they knew you would rock. They listened when you had complaints and assisted in resolving the issue. That leader got your attention, so they could ask more of you when they needed it. You also believed that the feedback they gave you was coming from the right place because of all the other truths and support you received from them.

I am also sure you have experienced a leader who never showed any vested interest in you. They never complimented you or asked you how your family was doing. They never asked you how you were enjoying your job or the project you were working on. When you complained, they tuned you out or did nothing about it. They probably yelled a lot or criticized you without care for your efforts. That leader likely got the bare minimum from you.

Now replace that leader with a friend, relative, in-law, brother, sister, or co-worker. How are you treating them? Are you investing in those around you on a consistent basis, or are you taking from them all the time? Are you draining the accounts of the people around you, or are you adding to them? Understand that investing in the accounts around you does not mean that each account will pay you back, but it means that the world will.

Call it karma, luck, or just getting what you deserve, but bad people get bad back. Good people get good in return. The more you give, the more you will receive. The more you take, the faster you will run out of people to ask for the things you need. And when you do this, people will expect that the only reason you are calling is that you need something. That schtick gets old, and so the people you reach out to will eventually stop answering.

You don't want to reach out to people simply to get what you want from them. Make sure you are also contacting people to give them something of value. This could be a lead, a greeting, or it could be as simple as saying, "I was thinking of you. How are you doing?" The point is to make sure you are giving more than you are regularly receiving.

Giving has an internal effect as much as an external one. Many people struggle with finding the balance of how much to offer. You may be afraid of getting taken advantage of due to previous experiences.

If that is the case, you are giving for the wrong reasons, or you are giving to the wrong people. A good rule of thumb to follow is that you need to provide more than you feel comfortable with at the moment you give. Do not stop at basic giving back. You will find when you give more than the minimum, the internal blessing both for you and the person or people you gave to is beyond compare.

I learned that lesson way too late in life. I was bullied a lot as a kid, which made me standoffish to people in general. So, I was never willing to open up and share or invest in others. I was gun shy. Once I became comfortable with who I was, no matter what others thought or said, I started building much better relationships because people knew the real me. Allowing myself to be true to who I was on the inside brought internal happiness and joy that no one else could have ever given me. This also goes a long way in growing as a person over time, and it creates tremendous external happiness.

Giving does a lot more than just help others. It also makes you feel better, which has a snowball effect on your feelings, mood, personality, and general likability. These are all traits that make you a more natural person to grow a relationship with—because better understanding yourself allows others to understand you better.

Your ability to grow healthy relationships is the difference between getting ahead and feeling like you are stuck in the same place, at the same level forever. Focus on how you are investing in those around you, and you will see incredible changes in how they invest back.

The Rule of Reciprocity is incredibly powerful, and I am going to dig even deeper into it in the next chapter.

CHAPTER 10

THE RULE OF RECIPROCITY

There is one word that may serve as a rule of
practice for all one's life—reciprocity.
—Confucius

WHAT IS RECIPROCITY?

Reciprocity is sometimes referred to as the Rule of Reciprocity; it is a social norm where if someone does something for you, you then feel obligated to return the favor.[3]

Doing for others is one of the most undervalued activities between people. But despite people not giving back as much, people talk about bringing value to others a lot! You have heard it, I am sure, at some point in the past. Few hold themselves to consistently providing as a part of their routine.

I hope to shed some light on the power of this activity and how to go about making it happen in your life so you can start to benefit from the power and success it can bring you!

I have talked a lot about relationships and approaches,
but very few of my actions have paid me back
as much as giving to others in my career.

As I have begun to experience more success through using influence and financial giving, it has become a big part of what fulfills me. Being personally

---

[3] "What is Reciprocity?" Very Well Mind, accessed July 1, 2021, https://www.verywellmind.com/what-is-the-rule-of-reciprocity-2795891#what-is-reciprocity.

fulfilled and grateful for what you have is the true underlying benefit of giving without expecting in return. It allows you to be thrilled with what you are doing.

I told someone the other day that I work so hard to get what I have because I want to give more.

But I typically hear people asking where to give, what to give, and how to give. They are usually afraid of investing time, money, and energy in the wrong opportunities. The trick around this that I have found is to give at all times.

HELP FIRST

One of my company's core values is "Operate with a Help First Mentality." It looks like this:

- Uncover and solve problems as the top priority
- Use a no-sales sales approach
- Look for opportunities to add value
- Give without expectations

You'll notice I have included nothing like, "Only give if the situation is correct." Or "Only give if that person can bring you value in return."

You have to give regardless, and here is why.

You never know when, how, or who is going to bring that value back to you.

Seeding a new yard at your house is similar to how your market works. It starts as bare dirt and is ugly and unusable, bringing you no value. You wouldn't go out and plant seeds one at a time based on their likelihood of taking root and growing grass.

You would go out and toss seeds all over the place, knowing that enough will take to grow a fully lush yard. If you tried to be selective about which seeds went down and where and when they went, you would have one messed-up-looking yard.

But just throwing them out on the ground and hoping they grow is not enough either. You have to water all the seeds with the same amount of water and at the same time. You can go out and carry a hose and walk around and water all the sections of the yard. Think of this as a hands-on networking approach. You can also set up a sprinkler on a timer to regularly water the seeds to make sure they get the water they need, which is similar to a structured and consistent automated or outsourced approach. Both methods can be effective, but we know you are not hitting the lawn with an eyedropper and deciding which seed gets water and which doesn't based on its potential to bring you what you want!

Now, look at your network of people! Have you been selective of who you are willing to do things for? Have you been selective on which calls you take or which DMs you respond to? If so, I bet you are not getting much value regularly either.

When you simply give, you have to accept that you may never hear back from that person. Still, I promise you that if you are consistent, things will happen for you in ways you cannot explain and that I cannot explain.

Not all people are created equally. You already know this, but you probably still let it affect you. I see this happen with people in their sales process, their follow-up process, and their marketing approach. If they get one lousy response, they begin to change everything about their system or method to try to get a different reaction or response from that same person next time. As you can imagine, changing everything you do regularly will not have the intended effect you want because of the lack of consistency for you and the audience.

Let's not forget, some people out there are takers. They drain everything around them and then move on to a new location and start all over again.

You know the person in your life who I am talking about—the person you see at a new company all the time. Or you might see them visiting a recent networking event, or they've enrolled in a new mastermind group *again*, blaming the last place for not being valuable enough for them to stay around. That is the most significant sign of a victim mindset that drives me up a wall.

Take some ownership of your success, and you might find it.

Don't let people who don't practice good habits stop you from investing in and focusing on bringing value to the people around you who do care about the quality of their relationships. It is ultimately a sign of your character as much as theirs when you are always the one others see as giving back and helping those around you level up to get what they need in their life.

Just like people can see a taker from a mile away, they can also see a giver as quickly.

There is a dichotomy to this fact as well. Some people will give to you and expect something in return. Some people will only take the time to give to people who they suspect will give something back to them. Some will ignore those who they don't think they can get value from. These interactions happen all the time, so it is essential to ask questions to determine what type of person you are dealing with in the moment. A simple, "Dude, that is awesome, thank you, what can I do to support you?" can uncover and avoid giant gaps in expectations.

The most significant fact to remember is that reciprocity can work for you and against you.

I am notorious for having an active bitch face. Contrary to a resting bitch face, you can tell what I am thinking and feeling at any given moment without me needing to say much. I didn't always realize how impactful this was to the people around me.

I am often distracted with an issue, or I am tired and hangry, which I express badly. In the worst-case scenario, I am the perfect storm of tired, hangry, and distracted, and you better stand back, throw some food at me, and wait for me to recover. DO NOT APPROACH THE BEAST DURING THESE SCENARIOS. (Haha!)

People didn't understand my feelings, and what drove me to have the expression on my face. They took how I looked and responded personally. Not that they were wrong to do that, but it was not my intent to direct my internal issues at them. When this happens, people start to pay you back with the same temperament to make you "feel" how you made them feel.

People will start to be short with you, avoid you, talk bad about you, and try to make you pay for the way you treated them. Perception is everything, and the truth is in the eye of the beholder. If people do not know what is going on in your head, they will make up a story about what is going on, and 100% of the time, it will be incorrect—because they cannot know the truth about you unless you tell them. Projecting your negative internal issues can lead to hatred, frustration, disappointment that you did not intend to cause, but you will still be paid back 10x just the way a great person is paid back. Be very mindful of how you look, speak, and interact when you are not feeling it because if you cave in to your emotions, it will incite those around you to pay you back what you invested in them!

I have learned this lesson time and time again and have gotten better, but I still struggle sometimes with wearing my emotions on my sleeve. Now, I try to recognize it more as I strive to be more intentional with how I am communicating when I am not really in the mood. I suggest you learn to catch yourself in the moment and pivot, too, so that you do not see waves of negative reciprocity coming back to you.

How do you go about making this happen for you?

How do you start to be intentional with your actions so you can reap the benefits of the Rule of Reciprocity?

GETTING INTENTIONAL

First, find someone in your ecosystem who seems to be winning all the time!

Do you know anyone in your life who seems to Win Fast and Win Often, who wins so much that you cannot understand how those wins keep coming to them?

You might even think they are just lucky and get the best opportunities. I will tell you from experience if you are consistently looking for ways to add value and go above and beyond for others, gratitude and blessings will come back tenfold regularly!

Be the first one there, the last one to leave, and the one who does the most without expectations, and you will become a leader that people will value and emulate. Period!

I have covered many ways to add value and be there for people already, but here are a few examples of how you can bring value to people who will help you build your social capital.

BUILDING SOCIAL CAPITAL

One of the best things you can do to build social capital is support and invest in organizations or causes that other people feel strongly about making successful. Maybe it's a fundraiser or an event that is important to someone in your sphere of influence. It's cool to share it and comment about how wonderful it is, but what if you took an active approach to help them raise funds or donate yourself?

What if you volunteered at their event or connected them to someone with a more significant influence than you who could help them gain traction for their cause?

After I started the nonprofit A Champion's Shoes in 2020, the people who donated stood out to me more than those who simply congratulated me because of the amount of sacrifice it took on their part to go to the webpage, fill out the info, and donate their hard-earned money. The more significant the sacrifice, the larger the impact.

The people who showed up to help wrap shoes or those who helped write cards didn't spend any more than others; they decided to donate their time. Time is also a massive gift that is more valuable to me than money. If you know me, you know my schedule is constantly slammed. It is a lot easier for me to donate money than time. So, when I give my time, it is a much larger sacrifice, which is why I appreciate those who help hands-on.

Because the cause is so important to me, when someone went out of their way to sacrifice their time or money to make my vision come to life, it stood out in my mind. Anyone involved with the charity also noticed their participation, and that generated more recognition and new connections. These people might never have made those connections if they hadn't given without expecting anything in return.

Since then, I have donated to eight to ten causes that I would not have even thought about before—and all because I owed people reciprocity. I have also supported another local organization and donated 100 pairs of shoes there. The son of the man who runs that effort became a coaching client of mine. I would not have met that person otherwise. I did not donate to gain a client for my coaching business, but it happened because I went out and gave, so the value came back to me in an unexpected way.

ADDING WOW TO SOMEONE'S LIFE

Another way to stand out and gain respect is to give unexpected WOW experiences or deliverables for people. I give in a multitude of ways, but three stand out that you can make your own.

Client Gifts

First, I give my clients gifts twice a year. I have sent a little something to clients unexpectedly with the intent to add value for as long as I can remember. In the summer of 2020, I sent hats with a handwritten note to every client I've ever had—not just the ones in 2020. Again, the more effort and the larger the time investment, the more impactful it is. People know it takes time to write out 100-plus cards, so when they get a card, it shows how much I appreciate them. Doing this is a way to show gratitude as well as understand my clients.

At the end of the year, I sent leadership and marketing books that were of value to everyone. Almost any business could benefit from reading them. As a business coach, giving people educational value matches what I do for a living, and it matters to those who are actively trying to get better. (You are likely reading this book as a gift, so thank you for being a part of the WinRate Family!)

Buying the books, organizing them, packaging them in branded boxes, putting a custom note on the first page of each one, and shipping them all took time, effort, and money. My customers knew this, and so it planted seeds of appreciation that keep me top of mind as well as it made my clients feel like they owe me one.

If you have thought of doing this, but haven't yet, don't use this excuse: "But I don't have everyone's addresses." Just ASK!

Newborn Gifts

The second thing I try to do as often as I can is send new parents a newborn gift package. Any parent knows of a few products that made life easier with their new baby. For my wife and me, it was glow-in-the-dark pacifiers and perfect swaddle blankets. Every time I see someone in my network have a baby, I jump into their DMs, get their address and send them the same items we used with our boys through Amazon. It might be only $40 worth of stuff, but it could be what impacts them the most in helping them get through those long nights. Or it might help them find that paci without having to turn on the lights—so they don't further upset their screaming baby! Trust me: the glow-in-the-dark paci is a life-changer!

Make Birthdays and Holidays Personal

Third, when someone has a birthday, or there is a major holiday, I send them a DM, make a phone call, or shoot them a text. It's more direct than just writing on their wall. Most people get hundreds of people posting on their wall. But it is hard to keep up with all those messages, and they end up blending together. But a personalized phone call or text message from you sticks out these days. I also highly suggest doing this because you don't know who is dealing with what and who needs to hear a friend's voice. This gesture can go a long way in making a significant impact in a person's life and in helping them get through a tough time.

I have even gone as far as to record a quick selfie video to thank them for something they have done for me or tell them how proud I am of them for what they have done. A quick video saying happy Thanksgiving, Merry Christmas, or happy birthday goes a lot farther than a standard greeting on their Facebook wall.

I am not 100% successful in hitting everyone in my life with these messages, so if you didn't get one from me, it is not personal! I get busy like everyone else. Although I try hard to focus on making these gestures regularly, it feels good to make someone's day, and it helps you stand out as someone meaningful and important to them.

You have to look outside yourself to add value to others who will pay you back over time. Trying to trudge through life only focused on yourself is an arduous path. So go out TODAY and find someone you can add value to without expecting anything in return. Even try to do it anonymously to make sure there is no way they can pay you back.

- Send that happy birthday video.

- Send a handwritten card.

- Donate to a cause. (achampionsshoes.org. Wink!)

- Go above and beyond to support someone else in an initiative or organization important to them. You may surprise yourself with how quickly what you have done comes back around and brings someone into your life who can fill a gap or solve a problem you have been trying to figure out on your own!

CHAPTER 11

BECOMING INTENTIONALLY SUCCESSFUL

It was character that got us out of bed,
a commitment that moved us into action,
and discipline that enabled us to follow through.
–Zig Ziglar

It's been five years since I stopped selling remodeling work, and I still get calls from people asking to work with me because they can trust that I give honest and straightforward feedback. They can trust that I said I would do what I said I was going to do. I sold millions of dollars' worth of construction projects with zero experience because I followed through on what I said I would do.

Just committing to that initially put me miles ahead of most of my competition. Most customers would say things like, "I called six people, and you're the only one who called back!" Or "I have been waiting five weeks for an estimate after he said he would send it in a few days."

If you can't get that part of the process right and done on time, why would anyone trust that you could properly handle managing their project to completion on time and effectively?

The way people respect you and take you seriously has a lot to do with external benefits. If you want to be trusted, you have to be someone who can set proper expectations and follow through on them. We will dig into more tactics and strategies later in this chapter, so make sure to keep reading.

THE TRUST FACTOR

The trust factor is not just external. Your ability to grow confidence and belief and trust in yourself is directly related to how well you follow through on what you tell yourself to do!

Nothing grows self-belief faster than committing to doing something, planning for it, preparing for it, and executing it to completion!

There are three phases to this process:

1. **Plan**: understand what you are trying to accomplish, when you want to achieve it, and with whom.

2. **Prepare**: research, organize, and schedule the information, tasks, and data you need to accomplish and by when.

3. **Execute**: follow the game plan to completion.

In my opinion, it is this simple! But we find ways to complicate this process regularly.

One of my biggest driving fears that helps me to accomplish what I need to is regret. I worry about the guilt of the things I didn't do.

When my anxiety and depression cropped up in my life, it had to do with the fact that I had not been committed to the game plan and following through for myself. I knew that I was not following through on what I needed to do or didn't need to be doing anymore. Our conscience and internal self-talk are impressive, especially when you are not listening. They can trigger all kinds of emotions!

The pain of anxiety is your body telling you that you are off the path and not following through on your commitments to yourself. Period!

Just like your body tells you that calmness, confidence, and self-belief mean you are listening well, the flip side is true when you hold out on yourself.

I wish I understood the simplicity of this and recognized how much I could be my own worst enemy. I know what excuses to concoct for myself. I know the exact details of what to say in my head to give myself a break. I know exactly how to create false scenarios and situations that justify giving up or giving in early. So, I should know the reality of the effects I cause to make my life harder.

Here are some examples of how people cut themselves breaks when they shouldn't:

- You worked hard; you deserve this cheat meal.

- It's just one drink a week, which turns into one glass a night.

- You are better than most people you know.

- You are winning enough. Don't worry about that mistake.

- You always deliver on time; this one time won't matter.

- I don't need to prepare for this; I will be fine.

LIES!!! All LIES!!!

These are the excuses you use to convince yourself it's okay to slack, but your mind, body, and soul know the difference. It knows when you ACTUALLY did the work. When you ACTUALLY did your best. When you ACTUALLY followed through to completion.

Even when you take some action and get 99% of the way there but don't finish, your body knows. It will tell you in brutal ways that what you did wasn't ideal—especially when you keep ignoring it.

You don't even need to slide on the big things to feel this impact. The little things that seem insignificant can eat away at you, too.

Like …

- Not finishing the dishes 100%

- Not finishing the laundry 100%

- Not finishing your reps at the gym 100%

- Cutting your workouts short

- Cutting your prospecting time short

Cutting corners on anything, no matter how little, will erode your confidence. Once you commit to yourself or others, you *have* to see it through!

**Besides, if you can't do the little things right,
how can you possibly do the big things well?**

Like putting the cart back at the grocery store.

Cleaning up after yourself.

Responding to people who call, email, and text you. (You know, even as you are reading this, there is someone you meant to call back and have not yet.)

Hitting self-imposed deadlines.

Posting once a day on social media. ("But Mike, I don't know what to post?!?" If you need more help on this, check out my Inking Wins Social Media Training Program that can be found at www.winrateconsulting.com.)

Even closing your locker at the gym when you leave.

(I come into the locker room six days a week to find half of the doors open. It's a simple task, but people push the door open and walk away whether it closes or not. It may seem minor, but if you are always leaving things "almost done," why do you think you would complete any of your targets or initiatives?)

There needs to be a non-negotiable line in your life of if you will do something or not.

Not "good enough!"

Not "better than most!"

Not "almost done!"

Do the absolute best you can every day, and you'll experience feeling like you are on the outside of success less.

There is a fee to get what you truly want in life. And it's 100% effort 100% of the time.

It's putting 100% of your best effort into anything you do and leaving it all on the field.

Sit down today and ask yourself, *what am I settling for as standard in my life, and what will I adjust the bar on today?*

BE AWARE OF THE FOLLOWING WHEN PROPERLY FOLLOWING THROUGH

The key to proper follow-through is setting appropriate expectations!

If you constantly tell people, "I will get something back to you ASAP," you are your own worst enemy.

If you find yourself saying that to dozens of people at a time, there is no way for them or you to know when that expectation will be met. When you do this, you paint an unrealistic picture of a five-minute window you might have tomorrow. As you say this, you also know your response time damn well never actually plays out that way.

The real issue is that the other party sets an expectation of what ASAP means to them. It could mean that afternoon, the next day, the following week. It's all variable, but that doesn't change the fact that it's a fictitious end date and that by choosing that date and not delivering, you leave doubt in the recipient's mind on your ability to deliver anything else. As you can imagine, this reduces your ability to build trust with the people around you.

I am sure you know someone in your life who is habitually late. Whether it's an event, a dinner, a movie, or a call back, that person is never on time and can't be trusted. Then what happens when you need something done right or on time? You call someone else.

You don't hate that person.

You probably don't even say anything to them about it because they always show up with some bullshit excuse about why they are late, but that doesn't change the way you feel about it.

Don't be that person, and you will find that the people around you will call you when they need help. Most of the time, that critical task that someone needs from you is a simple problem for you to solve. This gives you the ability to bring a lot of value with less effort allowing you to have a higher earning potential.

Why do you think some salespeople have more success than others with the same service or product in the same market even if they charge more? It is not because they find better clients. It's because they are better at following through, which makes them more trustworthy and valuable.

So, how do you go about making sure you are not that person, or how do you stop being that person? (You know who you are!)

Step one: you have to understand when, where, and how you will get your priorities done.

MY TWO SECRET WEAPONS

My process hinges on two critical rules. The first is time blocking my calendar, and the second is a task manager application that I use religiously.

I use the calendar app Fantastical and the task management app Asana. You can find a complete video breakdown on my YouTube channel, *Mike Claudio*, in the video titled "How to Have a Work-Life Balance."

When you watch the video, you will understand I hold the belief that there is no such thing as work-life balance. You cannot put equal efforts into every part of your life and get enough done. You have to put the right amount of effort into each part of your life.

When I think about the work-life balance, an old baseball saying comes to mind: "You have to know what you are going to do with the ball before it gets hit to you."

You can apply that saying to your life as it pertains to managing the inputs that come into your life. Do you get texts, calls, emails, DMs, drop-ins, letters, and maybe even faxes? (Is that still a thing?)

Regardless, you must have a strategy to keep up with it all because the person on the other side does not care about how busy you are or what else is going on in your life. They need a response from you, and they expect you to deliver.

This is the mistake I see most people make. The person making the request does not need an answer right his second. They need to know you have received their request, what the next step is, and when it will happen. That is impossible to do if you do not have a sound and organized calendar and plan for your days.

A simple explanation is PLENTY: "I got your request, plan to look at it Thursday afternoon, and will have something back to you Thursday night or Friday morning."

You have to understand that others' priorities do not automatically become your priorities. You have to control your time to put the right amount of time into all aspects of your life. So, having follow-up time at the end of every day for 30 minutes to get back to people and letting them know when you plan to get to their request is far better than pencil whipping a response together that you already know you cannot deliver on.

Sure, taking this tactic means you will upset some people—especially those who are used to you jumping in and helping whenever they ask, especially employees. But I would rather upset you with a realistic and honest expectation than let you down with a false one.

That is how you become known as someone who can be trusted and who will do what you say you will. That is when people start to appreciate you and come back when they need a real and honest answer.

Think about how many people have said to you, "I found someone to get to it quicker." Many times, that person ends up calling back because the provider they chose didn't deliver on what they promised, and now they need someone to do what they say they will. Since you were honest from the beginning, you now have a reputation as someone who will do what they say they will.

You also have to make it a priority to communicate proactively.

COMMUNICATE PROACTIVELY

Do you even know what that means? I didn't realize it at first.

In short, people should never have to ask for new or changed information from you to make an educated decision.

When I trained my sales teams, one of my biggest priorities that I made sure people followed through on was addressing their lateness or absences. If you were ever going to be late to a meeting, you needed to call and communicate that as soon as you realized it. I didn't care if you were one minute late. This rule still holds true today. If you are late, everyone involved with you needs to know that.

I'd rather sit there and wait an hour for a meeting to start than have clients or prospects wait a minute. If you provide no notice, then just know that the other person always has an opinion and will tell themselves a story about why you are late. And it's never a positive story. I became known as the guy who was always early and always prepared. That way, when I did call with a delay, it was a rarity and not the standard experience of working with me.

I constantly communicated if I even thought I would be late with a quick text message or phone call. It completely changed the experience of the other person. So, I still adopt this methodology for my days.

True masters of communication do what so many people are afraid to do. You have to be willing to take the first step to discuss what is going wrong or what might upset someone or even lose you the deal, project, or contract.

When things are not going the way you expect, that is when it is most important to let people know what's really going on. When you are strong enough and willing enough to proactively face people with bad news, you will gain 100% respect from those involved due to the fact that this is something so few people do.

Many hope that issues won't come up or be recognized. I have seen people sit on important info and feel accomplished if they didn't get caught or if no one ever found out. Well, I'm sorry to tell you, but people almost always find out, and if they believe that you knew about a complication or snag in the project before they did, you will lose that trust, friend, or even family member immediately.

I'd rather someone hate me for the truth than love me for a lie!
– SAY THAT TO YOURSELF AGAIN.

When you hit lows in your life, you need the people you care about to be around. Whether it's a sales slump or a dark place in your life, having people love you for the right reasons makes it easier for them to help you when you need it most.

At a high level, communicating proactively means thinking ahead and anticipating what's coming so you can intentionally communicate what's needed.

THE COMMUNICATION BREAKDOWN

This approach is one of the core values in my business, WinRate Consulting. I am a business coach primarily focused on helping people with sales and leadership. I teach that the ability to communicate proactively is incredibly important —because it is. It moves you forward and is a critical skill.

Here is how to Communicate Proactively:

- Set proper expectations
- Plan ahead to problem-solve proactively
- Learn when expectations change
- Take ownership and accountability of your tasks

The goal is to improve communication around deliverables and expectations.

If someone expects something from you and needs some help or information to complete the task, bring it up! Ask the question.

If you get hit with an issue or problem on a project or initiative you are in charge of, be resourceful. When you present the problem, offer a solution.

This means that when you see a potential issue or concern, you take the initiative to become part of the solution and help bring the project home.

It also means being intentional about your wins. Often in business and life, we are so distracted by our issues that the only time we talk to people, like our kids, spouse, or employees, is when they are doing something wrong.

You have to be proactive with praise just as much as correction, or you will end up looking like an ungrateful leader. We get into our heads and assume the people around us know what we are thinking but rarely do we communicate about the good with as much passion as we do the bad. When we do this, we wind up leading people to feel like we don't want, need, or appreciate their help. You can see how this would be a negative force in whatever you are trying to accomplish.

Schedule time on your calendar or in your meeting agendas to be grateful for what people around you are doing. It will come off as very proactive and unexpected, which will significantly impact that person!

Remember, following through means having a no-excuses mindset. You cannot have tolerance for excuses if following through is a priority to you.

We have internal and external forces working against us at all times, and the minute you begin to believe it all as truth and reality, you will lose.

Circumstances are never as good or as bad as you think they are, so stop letting them get in your way from accomplishing the promises you have made to yourself and others. I could probably write an entire chapter on just that topic alone but let me state that the following are insights I have learned about listening to excuses.

To follow through on achieving anything you commit to, you have to get out of your comfort zone.

So, by definition, following through is going to be uncomfortable.

Learn to recognize the discomfort as growth and lean into it. If you start to believe the waves of discomfort that you feel are a failure on your part, you will get stuck at the shore.

Instead, push forward, put your head down, ignore the uncomfortableness, and continue to advance. You will end up seeing an open sea of possibilities and accomplishments.

Once you begin to gain traction on the goals and initiatives you want to accomplish, you will get a lot of pushback from people around you. Some will try to help you, and others will try to slow you down. You have to believe in why you are doing something, so your lighthouse can guide you.

The people who love you don't want to see you hurting, so they will try to stop you from pushing too hard or too far, believing you are at risk of hurting yourself.

The people who don't like you hate to see you win, so they will also try to slow you down. They will think about how they couldn't have what you are going for and that you don't deserve it. They will plant distractions in your head.

Your why and the impact of accomplishing your goal has to be more significant than any excuse you could come up with that could stand in your way.

People ask me all the time how I stay so disciplined, consistent, and get so much done. My answer has always been the same. My goals are bigger than my excuses, so I have no choice but to ignore them.

Focusing on goals over excuses gets me out of bed at 3:55 a.m. and has helped me create podcast content for three years and almost 1,000 videos. The excuses are short-term and irrelevant compared to the impact I want to make, so I let them roll off.

You are no different.

If you let the excuses stop you from doing the work and taking action, you will not accomplish what you want to do. Additionally, you will let down those who need you to step up and Win Fast and Win Often.

Don't get me wrong; I am not saying I never have negative thoughts or face tasks or chores I don't want to do. I choose to ignore the thoughts because doing the work is more important to me than ease of life and comfort in everything I do.

Plenty of people talk about being successful and elite.

Few actually do anything about it, and even fewer follow through.

Which side of that equation do you want to be on?

CHAPTER 12

THE FORTUNE IS IN THE FOLLOW-UP

*Diligent follow-up and follow-through will set you apart
from the crowd and communicate excellence.*
—John Maxwell

You have probably heard all the different follow-up phrases in the past.

- FU Money is in the follow-up.

- The gold is in the follow-up.

- The fortune is in the follow-up.

- Even follow up Friday.

Whatever you have heard, here are some cold hard facts for you to understand how important and profitable having a follow-up game is!

It takes an average of eight cold call attempts to reach a prospect.[4]

- 2% of sales happen on the first contact

- 3% on the second

- 5% on the third

- 10% on the fourth

- 80% on the 5th-12th contact

Now, this next stat might surprise you because EVERYONE says it takes multiple touches to close a deal. But only 8% of salespeople follow up more than five times.

---

[4] "130 Eye-Opening Sales Statistics for 2021," Spotio, accessed July 8, 2021, https://spotio.com/blog/sales-statistics/.

That means 80% of sales go to 8% of salespeople.

Eighty freaking percent.

If you want to Win Fast and Win Often, follow up consistently, and you will come out ahead of 92% of your competition just by outlasting them in the contact game.

That is why those future touches are so important.

I have seen anywhere from 3-7% of any market actively looking to buy now while 40% are preparing or researching, and 50% are not ready at all.

So, if you're waiting for people to call you back when they are ready, you are fighting for 2% of sales made on the first call of the 3% of your market ready to buy.

If you have been struggling to close sales, it may make more sense to you why it is crucial to have a structured and needed follow-up process.

Let me explain.

FIRST TIME FOLLOW-UP IMPACT

The first-time follow-up ever impacted me positively was right after I failed out of college and was looking for a job.

Chris' Lawn Care was hiring a laborer, and I knew one of the guys who worked there, so I applied. We talked over the phone, and he said he would get back to me by the end of the week.

Well, he didn't, so I followed up every two to three days for almost three weeks until he called me back and said, "Anyone willing to follow up that many times has to get the job!"

I honestly was only following up because I was living on my parent's couch, and I needed a job badly, but that lesson stuck with me for a long time. The first time I heard someone tell me: "Anyone who would follow up that many times wins," I knew following up was something I had to be great at to win consistently.

Whether it was my job at Verizon, the remodeling company, the roofing company, or in any of my several businesses, follow-up has always been crucial to my performance.

At one point, I calculated that more than 40% of my construction sales over five years were directly related to follow-up activity. Overall, I did somewhere between $10-12 million in sales, which is an instant $4 million-plus in revenue from follow-up.

If you look at it from the other person's perspective, also known as empathy, it all makes a lot more sense.

FOLLOW-UP IS EMPATHY

Likely that prospect is a top priority because you are trying to get value from them, but you are unlikely to be their top priority.

They have jobs and lives and families and distractions.

They have priorities, and issues pop up.

They have a hundred things coming at them, and you are at the bottom of their list to call back.

It is your job to guide them to your solution so they can overcome their problem.

Knowing how to bring value to actual problems is a topic probably best reserved for a whole other book. But if you do not believe what you are offering will solve your prospect's issues, it is tough to get behind it. In other words, you have to believe that your solution will benefit your client.

Now more than ever, people who I follow up with to sign them up as a coaching client thank me down the road for being persistent in helping them make the decision. If you are missing that commitment to bringing value to others, following up will feel like an interruption and nuisance, so you won't do it.

That is why the best salespeople in the world love following up with people. They know that if they do their job correctly, the prospect will be in a better place than if they don't do business with them.

More people appreciate being followed up with when it has to do with something they want. If you are just calling to check the box and beg them to take the sale without any perceived value, they will get frustrated with your calls. You will also hate making them. Don't forget: every goal revolves around providing value to your clients and prospects.

It wasn't always easy for me to remember to follow up. I had to create systems and processes to make sure I kept up with everyone who needed a touchpoint. Ever since I started WinRate Consulting, I have made social media posts every Friday related to #FollowUpFriday. That drilled the importance of following up into my head, too.

YOUR BLUEPRINT TO MY MILLION-DOLLAR CLOSEOUTS

Don't just read the rest of this chapter; study it, take notes, and implement what you have learned. I am going to give you the blueprint I have used to close millions of dollars in projects that have allowed my company and me to make an impact on thousands of lives.

The First Follow-Up Step

The first and most important step you can take is to never, and I mean never, end a conversation without a defined next step and timeframe or deadline when you will talk to the person again.

It doesn't matter if it's a high-value client, your spouse, or a friend you barely like, get a date!

This can be as complex as saying, "I will get you the proposal on Monday. How long do you want with it before we talk again? Does Thursday at 11 a.m. work for you to discuss the next steps?"

Or "I will connect with you in six months to see how things are going!"

Almost always, when a person is frustrated or anxious, it is because we have missed or misunderstood their expectations, so people have no idea what will happen next. Get good at being detailed to help people understand your process.

Even if you are unsure about what needs to happen, ask the question, "So, where do we go from here?" Or "What would you like to see happen next and by when?"

Talking like this might seem weird at first, but once you improve in asking those questions, you will uncover how much easier it is to close people because of how you make them feel.

Following up with someone who wants to hear from you is obviously easiest. But what will you do when someone doesn't want to respond?

How will you handle the infamous ghosting of a top prospect who stops responding to you when you thought you had it in the bag? Even top-performing salespeople have endured this.

In this scenario, you did everything right. You showed up on time. You uncovered the person's needs. You brought a value-added solution to the table. Then you set the proper next steps and delivered them, but the person didn't get back to you.

When you are navigating this situation, you have to determine how vital that opportunity is to you. One of the biggest time-wasters I see some sales reps haggle with is when they keep going after the same opportunities instead of spending time looking for new and better ones.

We all know that one salesperson who doesn't close much and who is always complaining. You'll likely hear them say things like, "I have been emailing them, but no one is ever getting back to me."

That happens, but before you commit to a follow-up routine, you have to understand any follow-up activity could also translate into time spent prospecting for new opportunities. As is the case with anything in life, there is a dichotomy to the effort. You can't follow up as the ONLY way to get more; as a salesperson, you *have* to follow up. You need to make it part of your routine. But before you do, make sure whatever opportunity you are pursuing is worth it!

I am going to break down two separate follow-up routines. One is for a short decision period, and one is for a longer one. You can refer back to this information and use it in any sales situation requiring follow-up in any industry.

Follow-Up for a Shorter Sales Cycle

Some industries are more reactive by nature. In emergency work or other services, someone has to make a decision very quickly because they are reacting to a bad situation like water damage, a leaking roof, or a broken-down car. Because these decisions have to be made so quickly, the follow-up is a lot more front-heavy.

If someone doesn't respond to me after the first call, I will follow up twice a day for four days, then every other day for six days, and once a week for three weeks. The contact or "touch" can be done via phone call, email, DM, text message, or hell, even smoke signals. It truly doesn't matter how you connect with them. I usually focus on how we initially started the conversation. In today's world, prospects will reach out via DM, text message, email, web submission, or phone call. However, they connected with me, I will use as the primary follow-up type. This is how you meet them where they are and make it as easy as possible for them to reply to you. We always want to remove any barriers that would prevent people from connecting.

Follow-Up for a Longer Sales Cycle

For a longer sales cycle, such as an elective remodel or a real estate transaction, your follow-up process will be a little longer.

From the day the prospect stops responding, I decide when I will reach out based on when they told me they were planning to decide on an option. If they were a few months out, that's slightly different from them stating they might be a few weeks away from biting

The baseline follow-up structure for a longer sales cycle is:

- Daily for five days
- Weekly for a month
- Monthly for a quarter

Keep in the front of your mind that the follow-up should be about them. You want to help them hit their deadline. Make your contact to them about you fixing the problem they came to you to solve. When you follow up, you are assisting them through their decision-making process.

When you reach out to talk to them, resist using generic messaging like, "Just checking in and seeing if you had any questions."

That language doesn't bring any value to them. They are likely busy and distracted with their own stuff, so only follow up with communication that will bring them value.

Typically, by the fifth or sixth attempt, I will hit them with something along the lines of, "If you have made a decision to go another direction, no problem. But just let me know, and I will take you off my follow-up list."

That typically sparks an answer of some sort.

You will likely get one of the following answers eventually:

"Sorry it has taken me so long to get back to you but give me a little more time."

"Sorry it has taken me so long to get back to you, but we went another direction."

"Thanks for following up! Let's get going on this!" This one happens a lot more than you realize. It is where all the fortune in the follow-up comes from.

You can do a lot of following up manually, but current technology and systems can enable you to automate a lot of your messaging. Set people up to get standard touch throughout their decision process. It can work, but I am a bigger fan of personalized and direct contacts. This has worked best for me, so I have stuck with it.

Keeping Track of Communication

I use two main programs to keep up with all these activities: my CRM and Asana.

What is a CRM?s

CRM stands for client relationship management tool. It is where you store all your client data, your notes, contact info, pipeline, estimates, etc. It's a one-stop shop to keep up with all the moving parts of your business. It blows me away how many people do not have one in place for their business. I use Keap for the coaching company and Markate for the grading company. Different needs require different solutions.

Here's what I typically want to keep track of:

- When did a contact or conversation happen?
- What issue was discussed?
- What critical pieces of the story set me apart from the competition in my sales approach and proposal?
- What is stopping them from moving forward right now?
- What are the next steps?
- What is the decision/project timeline?

I like having a standard template of the notes or questions I need to get answers to. When you use a CRM and get organized, you and everyone on your team know what information is necessary, what touchpoints have already been made, as well as where a prospect is in their decision-making process.

If you do not truly understand the problem the client is having, it is impossible to set the proper value and differentiate yourself in a memorable way. People only spend money on what will solve their problems. The bigger the problem, the higher the value people place on it, which allows you to charge more to solve it.

Asana

Asana is a task management tool that I use to plan and centralize all the people I need to connect with. Since I use Friday as my primary follow-up day, when I need to follow up with someone in the CRM, I add it to Asana for the upcoming Friday.

These are not complicated tools, but they are highly efficient in keeping me focused and consistent in my follow-up game. They can do the same for you.

Overall, it is best if you determine what works best for you, but you do need to create *something* with structure and checks and balances to stay consistent. So, choose an application or tool and commit to using it. You can always switch to a different program that you like better down the road. For now, get started to maximize your process and sales.

CHAPTER 13

MENTORSHIP

If you want to go fast, go alone.
If you're going to go far, go together.
—Old African Proverb

It doesn't matter the industry, field, sport, or area of life; there is not a single elite performer who does not have a coach. Anyone who is at the top of the top likely has several coaches that focus on different areas of their life to achieve greatness.

But for some reason, so many adults out there grow an ego so high they can't see past it and believe the investment is worth it. They will hire extra coaching and tutors for their kids, but it doesn't seem worth it when it comes to achieving their own goals.

Once we reach a comfortable level of achievement, the thought of pushing further scares people out of the idea of doing more to pursue their goals. There is nothing like fear to stop you dead in your tracks even if you want to win more and at a higher level.

SIX FIGURES

I remember how the chase to make six figures as a kid was deemed the pinnacle of success. I got there at 24. For most of my mid-twenties, I made over $125,000 per year. I saw rooms with people between the ages of 30-60 in the same position I was in because they got comfortable and settled. They were so scared of losing the comfort and security they had that that they walked away from tons of money on the table because they couldn't see what would or could happen next if they just tried to do more!

I've seen so many adults who are almost fit but who never got the assistance to take the next step. I don't care what they tried to sell us in 2019, but dad bod is not okay, and being overweight and unhealthy isn't going to make you happy. Still, people settle for what they believe they are capable of.

People actually believe they can't have general happiness or personal success, or they believe they don't deserve these things. I was in this battle for a long time and almost lost it.

I was in these situations until I found a mentor or coach who had accomplished what I wanted and who helped show me the way I was stuck.

I was stuck when it came to earning a certain income, attaining a specific fitness level, or battling with a lack of fulfillment and happiness.

To get unstuck, all it took was finding and being around people who had accomplished what I believed I wanted and me asking for that help and paying to get it.

The first step in finding the right mentors is asking yourself where you want to be and what you want to accomplish!

DON'T JUMP THE GUN

Before you sign any contract or sign up for any course or mastermind, at least get a baseline for who you want to become or what you don't want in your life. So many people get stuck in the cycle of self-development. They go to every event and are in every mastermind group but never take action on what they are learning. This does more harm than good.

People who get stuck in that cycle feel worse and worse about themselves because they keep putting themselves in the correct rooms and around the right people, yet nothing changes. When this happens, they blame everyone around them for why they are not getting to where they want to go.

No matter what mentors or coaches you have, none of it will matter without dedicating time to doing the work.

When you know who you want to be and what you want, you can ask better questions and find someone who has personally accomplished what you want to do. This will give them the ability to mentor you from their personal experiences and to help you avoid the challenges and hurdles set up on that journey to accomplishment. Ideally, any mentor or coach you hire will help you avoid mistakes, make better-educated decisions, shorten the failure gap, and hold you accountable for the right work you need to be doing at the right time.

To my mind, there are three types of coaches and mentors. None of them are "wrong" or "bad." They all serve a different purpose to help you become the person you need to be to accomplish the targets you have set for yourself.

Also, different seasons of life will require different types of mentors.

What works right now and what got you to where you are might not be what you need to get you to where you are going.

THE THREE COACHES

The Theoretical Mentor

The theoretical mentor is highly educated and has learned a lot about concepts, systems, and processes but has no actual hands-on experience. This is similar to a business professor who has never owned a business. They are likely very knowledgeable but won't have the real-world experience to compare their theories to.

The Coach

The coach has learned what they are teaching by being *near* someone who has accomplished what you want. These people are typically good at understanding what you need to meet your goals, but they lack the personal experience of doing and accomplishing what you want.

A great example would be the assistant coach to Bill Belichick. Many teams have hired his assistant coaches as their head coaches, but few have had even close to the same success. They have many of the same mindsets and best practices but are still not as good as Bill.

The Accomplisher

The accomplisher has done what you want to do to become the best version of yourself. Think of a college quarterback hiring Tom Brady to mentor him to the next level. Tom has personally accomplished everything needed to make it to that next level that the quarterback is shooting for.

Figure out who it is you are looking for. There is no right or wrong answer because different support means different things at different seasons of your life and business.

There are four main things I look at when considering a coach or group to join.

FOUR MENTORSHIP CONSIDERATIONS

Who are the current clients of that program or coach? Do I respect, admire, and look up to these people?

I don't need every person in the group to be at that high level, but I want to know if there are a solid number of people who will help me level up. I want to know if there are people I would be proud to say I run with while growing.

I also try to analyze the bottom of the list. Who are they willing to do business with to help themselves ascend to the level I want? I am very cautious of who I put my name alongside. I don't want to be associated with people who do not represent my core values.

What are the core values of the coach or mentorship group? What do they believe in, and how do they represent those beliefs?

If I am going to hook myself to others' direction and guidance, I want to ensure our ships are headed in the same direction. This is no different than when I want to hire an employee. If the leaders are headed in a different direction than the candidate or member, you will grow a giant expectation gap that will be hard to overcome down the road.

Are the habits and routines of the leaders of that coaching program or mentorship group representative of living a lifestyle that aligns with how I spend my time and energy?

Do these people have happy and healthy lifestyles, relationships, families, and marriages?

Are they currently running a business or organization that is similar to or that aligns with the type of business or organization I want?

While taking outside perspectives from others is great and can be very helpful, it is crucial to be confident that the person you are considering as your prospective coach has similar experiences and approaches to living. Working with someone who has been through what you are headed through ensures that their perspective has had identical situations and experiences behind it.

Life is not about one category where someone is excellent at business but terrible in their health or family. I don't want to work with someone whose marriage is over and who most people hate. That is not the definition of success to me. I want to be a well-rounded and fulfilled person, so I make sure the people I spend time around have similar interests and routines to guarantee their success across the board.

IS THIS A PERSON OR GROUP I CAN BRING VALUE TO?

For me, giving is as vital as receiving—if not more important. Finding people I am excited to learn from and who I can bring value to is a priority to me. Whenever there is a one-sided relationship, it never lasts, so I am typically looking to invest in long-term relationships and friendships with these people. That being the case, I want to make sure I have something to bring to the table.

This want stems from being confident and humble. I know my strengths and weaknesses, so it is easy for me to be humble and to receive feedback while also being confident in what I do know. Being self-aware is a vital part of successfully getting mentored.

If you have any ego in these circumstances, you will end up turning into a victim because you will think that the group just couldn't help you. This is because you will actually refuse help—you will think you know better and don't need "advice." Then you won't get the results you want; hence you will blame your coach for your failings.

Once you feel like your ego is taking over, you have to check yourself because the fact is, there is always something to learn and likely to teach in every room. If you feel like there isn't, it is time to get out because you will become hostile and bleed your victim mindset all over the room. That is not fair to you, the other members, or the coach.

HOW MUCH HELP DO YOU WANT?

Once you have these four questions answered, you have to decide how much help you want.

Plenty of people out there want to help others for free. You can find industry experts or people in a similar industry who wish to provide advice. In these instances, you will likely be an afterthought for them as they have other priorities to tend to that will pay them. So be careful that you don't skimp on the coaching services you need in favor of other services that won't allow you to grow as much.

Paying for a mentor or coach is by far the most impactful way to create meaningful change.

And just like anything else, the more valuable the coach and content, the more expensive the fee. Many times, more costly programs bring a much higher value and return on investment.

I have learned through running low-cost mastermind groups, mid-level blended one-on-one and group training, and high-level one-on-one coaching that it is exhausting working with people who you pour into but don't do the work.

These people are looking for an easier way, not the right way. That is why pricing goes up. The people who are willing to pay for the higher ticket prices are serious about change.

When I first started coaching, I was charging significantly less than I do now. My customers did not take what I had to say seriously because it was not a big enough fee or investment to get their attention. As I have raised prices, I have gotten a higher caliber client who wants the help and who will do the work I ask them to do.

High-level mastermind groups can cost $10,000, $50,000, or even $100,000 a year because the coaches want the right people in the room just as much as the other members want the right people in the room. The highest and top performers in the business world don't want to spend time around people who don't have value to bring to the table. They spend a bunch of money to hang around like-minded people so they can collaborate on deals and learn from those who have done the work.

There is nothing wrong with lower-level stuff. It just comes down to what you want to get from it and how fast.

My one-on-one coaching is very hands-on, very accountability-focused, heavily action item-centric, and broken down into steps that guide you to the result you want. It is a different experience than a $97 online group or course.

I always have and still do offer a 100% money-back guarantee on my coaching contracts because I know I am going to put my all into helping people. If it doesn't work or the client doesn't get the value they want, I want to make sure they either get a return on their investment or get their investment back. It has been like that since day one, and 125-plus clients later, no one has asked for their money back.

Make sure your mentor or coach has some skin in the game, too. I have heard so many complaints about coaches who did not deliver, resulting in the customer being unsure as to what they got for their money. I knew I didn't want to be that guy, and I have worked my ass off to make sure of that.

One of the best ways to vet someone ahead of time is to check their content. Most of my clients heavily understand who I am and what I believe in through all my content areas. If you like what you see and hear through my content or what you have read in this book, I would love to work with you!

GET IN TOUCH!

If you like videos, check out *Mike Claudio* on YouTube.

If you are an audio person, look at *Big Stud Podcast.*

My IG is @winrateconsutling.

My Facebook Group is Construction Selling.

My website is winrateconsulting.com.

Anyone who wants to grow the right audience will need to have a heavy focus on value-added content, on creating entertaining and educational content for their specific audience on a regular basis that brings value to the problems of that audience. This will help their customer base feel confident that they are hiring the right person.

If you want to hear more about what my current offers are or how I can bring value to you or your team, shoot me a DM on Instagram, and we can set up a time to talk!

I hope you have enjoyed this book and found tremendous value that you can use to change your life and business to make it and you into the best version of yourself.

These systems and processes are put together from my personal experiences building up my mind, body, network, and myself to keep me alive. They not only saved my life but allowed me to thrive to the best of my ability. You have read about setting up your life for success by creating better time management practices. About fueling your mind and body properly to keep you sharp and ready for what the world throws at you on a regular basis. About putting yourself into the correct position around the right people to level up and become #TooStrong to be held back by the obstacles of life. And finally, about how to go about finding and vetting the right mentor and coach for you.

I believe that final step is the most important step in the process. A quality mentor can help you figure it all out before you go through the growing pains of learning on your own! That right there is worth the price of this book. You can move faster with better information and be held accountable for everything in this book. Clearly, I am the expert on this grouping of best practices because I have lived everything you have read here, and I would love to talk to you about how I can help you. Check out winrateconsulting.com and fill out the contact form, and we can talk!

All that is left is for you to take action!

Plan

Prepare

Execute

Win Fast and Win Often!!!

ACKNOWLEDGMENTS

Thank you to Tiffany for being my rock. Without you, I would not be who I am or where I am as a man, husband, father, leader, and mentor. You have been the biggest supporter of me, and more than I could have ever imagined was possible from a partner. I love doing life with you F&A!

Thank you to Ryan Stewman for not giving up along the journey of mentorship. This job is not easy, and if you had given up or given in to the FOA, I would not have had the experiences, confidence, or belief in the possibility of this book and the impact I make every day. You blazed the path, and I will gratefully support my mission to follow and create some of my own paths along the way!

To the GoonSquad. You all live your lives to the fullest and put so much into everything that you do. We are changing the world and making a huge impact. Most people just don't know it yet! But we will be a massive presence in this world not because we are better than anyone else but because we are willing to do the work others are not. You all keep me focused and pushing to keep up with the pack. Thank you for not giving up on yourselves at any point because it gives me permission to go all in, and that is something I will never be able to thank you enough for beyond living the same way!

ABOUT THE AUTHOR

Mike Claudio has spent the last 14 years not just selling products but learning how to go out and develop a business.

His sales and management career started in the retail industry with Verizon Wireless. He later worked in their Enterprise Sales Department. During his time in Corporate America, he was given some of the best training in the world and developed a passion for communication and the client experience.

While Mike's formal training is in the corporate setting, he's always been pulled toward smaller companies where he can work with entrepreneurs to help them bring big changes to grow their business.

Mike found his love and passion for the people, processes, and services of the construction industry when he was given the opportunity to work with New Leaf Construction, a residential general contracting business in Charlotte, North Carolina.

After helping to lay the foundation at New Leaf Construction, Mike looked for new opportunities with construction companies with even bigger growth plans. He landed at Daniel Enterprises, a commercial and residential roofing and siding company. In his first 12 months with the company, he brought in over $2 million in sales and helped the sales team to more than double their revenue year-over-year.

He has proven his systems and processes to Identify, Target, Qualify and Acquire clients' work. He is now the founder and CEO of WinRate Consulting, where he has helped countless people reach their goals. He also builds up-and-coming Champions through A Champion's Shoes, his non-profit organization that provides shoes for children in need.

Mike is an inspiring coach, an admirable friend, a successful entrepreneur, an extraordinary father, and an exceptional husband. He is consistent. He is loyal. He is strong. And he has found a way to use all these attributes and life lessons to pour into championship-worthy entrepreneurs.

Mike teaches what he knows through empathy, the ability to understand and share the feelings of another. This is one of Mike's greatest assets. Being able to understand what others are feeling has influenced his way of life. Every process he implements, every action he takes, every conversation he has is built around the question, "What impact will this leave?" Being an empath is not for the faint of heart, and someone who is strong enough to appreciate how others feel without bearing the load for them makes for an incredible person to have in your corner.

Mike instills the belief in everyone he meets that if you consistently do the work, the results will come. He truly believes you are capable and worthy of success; you just need to want it badly enough.

As he knows what it feels like to doubt this feeling of worth, he believes that each and every one of us is #TOOSTRONG to give in to that belief.

BOOKS I HAVE READ

2017

The Defining Decade by Meg Jay
The First Phone Call from Heaven by Mitch Albom
Vindicated by Jose Canseco
From This Day Forward by Craig Groeschel
Outliers by Malcolm Gladwell

2018

Networking Like a Pro by Brian Hilliard and Ivan Misner
Getting Naked by Patrick Lencioni
Start With Why by Simon Sinek
Natural Born Heroes by Christopher McDougall
Be the Bank by Benjamin Michael Lyons
Tuesdays with Morrie by Mitch Albom
Unbroken by Laura Hillenbrand
The 21 Irrefutable Laws of Leadership by John C. Maxwell
Jab, Jab, Jab, Right Hook by Gary Vaynerchuk
I Can't Make This Up by Kevin Hart and Neil Strauss
The Rise of Theodore Roosevelt by Edmund Morris
The Compound Effect by Darren Hardy
The Richest Man in Town by V.J. Smith
How to Win Friends and Influence People by Dale Carnegie
*The Subtle Art of Not Giving a F*ck* by Mark Manson
Grit: The Power of Passion and Perseverance by Angela Duckworth
The Girls of Atomic City by Denise Kiernan
You Are a Badass by Jen Sincero
Where Men Win Glory: The Odyssey of Pat Tillman by Jon Krakauer
The Book of Five Rings by Miyamoto Musashi
Leaders Eat Last by Simon Sinek

You Are a Badass at Making Money by Jen Sincero
The Devil's Chessboard by David Talbot
How to Make Shit Happen by Sean Whalen
Shoe Dog by Phil Knight
Think and Grow Rich: A Black Choice by Dennis Kimbro and Napoleon Hill
Creativity, Inc.: Overcoming the Unseen Forces that Stand in the Way of True Inspiration by Amy Wallace and Edwin Catmull
Expert Secrets by Russell Brunson
The If in Life by Rashad Jennings
He Will Guide You by Rev. Dr. John Diomede
Lamb: The Gospel According to Biff, Christ's Childhood Pal by Christopher Moore
Crushing It! by Gary Vaynerchuk
The American Spirit by David McCullough
Profiles in Courage by John F. Kennedy
Principles by Ray Dalio
Leadership Lessons: Warren Buffett by Will Peters
Discipline Equals Freedom by Jocko Willink
Tools of Titans by Tim Ferris
Extreme Ownership by Jocko Willink and Leif Babin
Born Standing Up by Steve Martin
Zero to One by Blake Masters and Peter Thiel
10% Happier by Dan Harris
The Hard Things About Hard Things by Ben Horowitz
Coaching for Performance by Sir John Whitmore
Dichotomy of Leadership by Jocko Willink and Leif Babin

2019

Fire and Fury by Michael Wolff
Give and Take by Adam Grant
Man Up by Bedros Keuilian
The Perfect Day Formula by Craig Ballantyne
Titan by Ron Chernow
Unstoppable by Craig Ballantyne

Can't Hurt Me - David Goggins
#Maxout Your Life by Ed Mylett
A Life Well Played: My Stories by Arnold Palmer
Building a StoryBrand by Donald Miller
Surviving Survival by Laurence Gonzales
All Marketers are Liars by Seth Godin
Purple Cow by Seth Godin
Relentless by Tim S. Grover

2020

F*ck Your Excuses by Ryan Stewman
Hardcore Closer by Ryan Stewman
Elevator to the Top by Ryan Stewman
Sell It and Scale It by Ryan Stewman
Get Sh*t Done by Jeffrey Gitomer
This is Marketing by Seth Godin
GCode by Ryan Stewman
Tactical Leadership by Jacko Willink
Fearhunters by Noah Elias
The Magic of Thinking Big by David J. Schwartz
Kick Ass by Ryan Stewman
Bulletproof Business by Ryan Stewman
Be a Man! Becoming the Man God Created You to Be by Lawrence O. Richards

2021 READING LIST

My goal is to finish 52 books in 2021.

Theodore Roosevelt: A Strenuous Life by Kathleen Dalton
As a Man Thinketh by James Allen
Traction by Gino Wickman
The Five Dysfunctions of a Team by Patrick Lencioni
The New One Minute Manager by Ken Blanchard, PhD and
    Spencer Johnson, MD

Mastering the Rockefeller Habits by Verne Harnish

Rocket Fuel by Gino Wickman and Mark C. Winters

Good Profit by Charles G. Koch

The Dream Manager by Matthew Kelly

Masters of Success by Don Morgan and Ivan Misner

Zapp!: The Lightning of Empowerment by William C. Byham, PhD
    with Jeff Cox

Never Split the Difference by Christopher Voss and Tahi Raz

Greenlights by Matthew McConaughey

Crushing the Day by Drewbie Wilson

The One Thing by Gary W. Keller and Jay Papasan

Essentialism by Greg McKeown

Life is Yours to Win by Augie Garrido

The Five Temptations of a CEO by Patrick Lencioni

StrengthsFinder 2.0 by Tom Rath

Winning by Shari Wenk and Tim S. Grover

Make Good Choices by Marc Zalmanoff

DISCLAIMER

This book is a truthful recollection of actual events in the author's life. The events, places, and conversations in this book have been recreated from memory. The names and details of some individuals or entities have been changed to respect their privacy.

The information provided within this book is for general informational, educational, and entertainment purposes only. The author and publisher are not offering such information as business, investment, or legal advice or any other kind of professional advice, and the advice and ideas contained herein may not be suitable for your situation. Any use of the information provided within this book is at your own risk, and it is provided without any express or implied warranties or guarantees on the part of the author or publisher.

No warranty may be created or extended by sales representatives or written sales materials. You should seek the services of a competent professional before beginning any business endeavor or investment. Neither the author nor the publisher shall be held liable or responsible to any person or entity with respect to any financial, commercial, or other loss or damages (including but not limited to special, incidental, or consequential damages) caused or alleged to have been caused, directly or indirectly, by the use of any of the information contained herein.

Made in the USA
Coppell, TX
25 August 2021

61185412R00107